AF428429

# THROUGH THE FIRE

T.A. BENSON

# Through the Fire

T.A. Benson

Published by: T.A. Benson

To my beautiful wife.

# TRIGGER WARNING

This book has sensitive material relating to:

- Abuse
- Harassment
- Gaslighting
- Bullying
- Trauma
- Death
- Suicide
- PTSD
- Violence
- Grief
- & More

Remember to practice self-care before, during, & after reading.

# PART I: FIRST WINTER

"Out of suffering have emerged the strongest souls; the most massive characters are seared with scars."
  – Khalil Gibran

# 1

October's end.

I remember everything about that day. It was the first time in a while that real levity felt possible. It was freezing—so cold that my leather shoes couldn't stop winter from biting through.

I wore freshly polished Aldo brown leather shoes, a dress shirt, tie, slacks, and a peacoat—dressed for a friend's wedding that would start after work. The socks that went with my shoes could never be thick enough for Colorado's freezing wind. None could really.

I looked at the strange, stone Human Resources (HR) building, which was a block away from the older, dilapidated hospital where I worked in Mountainton. The new replacement hospital, which was still being built in Wylde Town Falls nearby, was located miles away from here. I was sent there to wait in an office cubicle for news about the future of my new nursing job at this hospital, which belonged to the Health Care Organization or *HCO*, as we called it. I walked through the double, creaking doors of the HR building as the first snow began to fall.

I walked to the front desk and told a clueless young man that I was there to meet with Kelly, the senior nurse officer, at 3:45 p.m., per her instructions. He made a call to someone who directed him to someone else while telling me to "Hold on a sec."

"She's still on her way," he said. "She should be here in a minute."

I nodded and paced back and forth, standing in the foyer of the building, and staring into the snow fall on the street. Something felt wrong. Hollow. As if I already knew how this was going to go.

I'd moved across the country almost six years earlier, building a reputation as an ICU respiratory therapist before earning a coveted nursing scholarship—a bonus to HCO employees that wanted to fill the voids of the ever-growing nursing shortage. I had had the best time going to nursing school. When it was time to start duty as a nurse, I was assigned to a nursing unit I rarely set foot on.

This was atypical of nursing jobs. The scholarship deal guaranteed a job, but typically, there would be some sort of relationship between the prospective new graduate nurse and the manager or unit. I had that with four other units: the Medical ICU, the Surgical ICU, the Emergency Department, and the Step-Down, which was where patients go after they are stable enough to leave the ICU.

On my first day, I was made to feel unwelcome on That Unit when I met the young nurse manager for the first time. During my nursing orientation, I was assigned to two challenging preceptors who handled the beginning and end of my training.

Between those experiences, I worked with a man who became my greatest mentor. I also encountered some genuinely kind and intriguing nurses from whom I learned a great deal.

In my final weeks, I transitioned to the night shift under a preceptor whose main task seemed to be making me leave at the request of my manager. That was his only goal.

It was because of him that I found myself recommended to appear before the Nursing Evaluation Committee (NEC) due to alleged issues with my performance and conduct. I stood before the NEC, shared my truth, and presented my evidence. They concluded that I'd done nothing wrong—but the dread stayed. And then, I saw her.

She wore black, the kind sold in the most expensive stores at the mall—and carried a large Louis Vuitton bag with leopard-printed gloves to match. My heart was in my throat. I quickly scurried away, lest she see me, and I took a seat near the clueless receptionist's desk. I heard the door open and fall close, and I heard another open and close. This was followed by the sounds of clicking high heels ascending a staircase.

The next five minutes felt like five years—longer than the years I'd spent working my butt off for the hospital, longer than my two Iraq combat tours combined, and longer than anything I'd ever done. The receptionist's phone rang, and he answered it. "Kelly will see you now. You can go up."

I stood up and walked to the elevator. I don't know why I was procrastinating at this point, but I was. The doors opened, I entered, hit the antiquated button to carry me to her, and the doors closed. A few short seconds later, the doors opened again, and I was on a newer, nicer floor.

Like any horror film, when the doors opened, I saw her standing there. She raised her head, smiled an awkward and strained smile, and said, "Hi, Miles." Per her direction, I followed her to an empty office room, which no one else was using. It was a beautiful, but barren office that had a cold glow cast over it by the lights above. I sat down as she pulled a file from her bag and opened it.

Kelly avoided my eyes and focused on the neat stack of forms. I could hear the faint click of her manicured nails against the folder. She finally looked up, her expression unreadable. "Miles, thank you for coming in."

I nodded, swallowing hard. My throat felt tight, my heart was pounding in my ears.

She exhaled and said "So, we finally have your NEC results, and I'm here to give them to you since the patient services manager is busy with another meeting. So, the CEO has read and signed off on the NEC's recommendation on what to do moving forward."

I waited, the silence stretching between us like a chasm. She paused to look me in the eyes, and she looked back down at her papers as if she couldn't stand to look at me for very long. I sensed she had a touch of pain. "And they did recommend moving forward with separating you from employment. This will be effective on Veterans Day."

The words didn't register. I stared at her, searching for any sign of a mistake.

Her eyes were fixed on the papers, her lips pressed into a thin line.

A cold numbness crept over me. "So...that's it?"

She nodded, her voice barely above a whisper. "It's a non-adversarial separation. You will be paid out all your unused vacation hours. You have a few weeks until this is effective. If you'd like, you can do just about anything you want. You can show up to work and sit in your cubicle, or you could take these two weeks as vacation. Your record is and will remain clean."

"I see," I replied, though I had much more to say. We exchanged glances, and it was hard to believe that the person attempting to be friendly to me now was the same one who wrote this email:

*I am sending a request for the Nursing Evaluation Committee to review the probationary period of Mr. Miles Smith, RN. This request is based on his performance and conduct while employed on That Unit. During orientation, his performance did not meet the standard. Additionally, there was a specific act of misconduct reported, where Mr. Smith asked his preceptor not to report or document his performance deficiencies to management.*

This email proved how easily a lie could become punishment. The coldness of those involved left me perplexed. This was a far cry from how everything had begun.

Before joining this unit, I had received letters of commendation for my performance. My career in the Army was decorated, and I made the Dean's List at both colleges I attended. I even received the Excellence in Nursing Award in nursing school. Now, they were acting as if I couldn't so much as tie my shoes right, and I was being laid off.

Kelly took a breath before she spoke again, which startled me, because it seemed like she was frozen and holding her breath while I sat there stunned, in a trance. "Now, this doesn't mean you are not or never will be a good nurse someday."

I only nodded.

Kelly hesitated, then reached for a form. "I know this isn't what you wanted. I want you to know, this isn't a reflection of your character. Sometimes... these things just happen." She had this look on her face of true confusion stirred in with a sprinkle of what may or may not have been compassion. "Do you have any questions for me? Anything at all?"

"I honestly don't really know what to ask at the moment. You say this is like a lay off?"

"Yes," she said. "It's completely non-adversarial."

"Can you help me understand just what that means?"

She had that O-shaped mouth again as she started, "Well, it means that you were released from employment during your probationary period as a nurse for reasons that were non-adversarial or no reasons at all. It means it did not work out, or you left on your own. Your privacy is important to us. And... this will work out in your favor."

I gave her a puzzled look.

"With the scholarship," she explained. "Do not worry about paying us back financially or with service time for the scholarship. That would have only applied to you if you had resigned."

"I really... I had no... I mean this isn't how I planned for this to go at all. I wanted to retire here. There were so many things I wanted to do."

She put her lips together in a pouting shape. "You know, I don't think bad of you. I've been at this hospital for twelve years and...these things just happen sometimes."

I looked at her, anger and disbelief warring inside me. "Is there anything I could have done differently?"

She shook her head, her eyes finally meeting mine. For a moment, I thought I saw regret. "You did everything you could. Sometimes, it's just... not the right fit."

I sat silent and nodded again. I was already running late for the wedding. My wife was worried by now.

Kelly looked at me again with strange curiosity. "You must be in...just...shock," she said.

That's a damn fine observation, I thought.

"You know, nothing really shocks me here anymore. Nothing at all." I shrugged my shoulders, which felt heavy, having sunken into my chair like dead weights desperately trying to find a seat in the ground or at this point, a grave.

"Ha!" Kelly exclaimed. "You know, that's exactly how I feel so many times over here. I'm constantly just like 'what the heck is this?' I totally get it."

She had a smile on her face of appreciation. It seemed I had said something to liven her spirits or even please her. There was an eeriness to her thankful posture. She gave me a look up and down, which sent a cold chill down my spine.

She seemed to be searching for something else to say. "Well, do you have any more questions for me?"

"I don't think I do now, you know. I'm sure I may think of some later. My mind's honestly drawing blank." I was still stunned.

"Ah. I totally get it. I get that way too. Every time I think of something, it's usually like in the middle of the night in the shower when I'm washing my hair or something." She nodded as she talked. It was strange. She was behaving as if we were friends getting a coffee in the mall and talking fashion.

I clenched my fists, fighting the urge to shout, to demand answers. Instead, after a bit of awkward silence, I said "Well, thanks for letting me know."

She stood, extending her hand. "Goodbye and good luck, Miles."

I pulled the weight of the world up as I stood and softly shook her hand, her grip cool and impersonal. I couldn't say a word at this point.

Kelly gestured down the hall. "Head through that door—there's someone from HR waiting to explain every-thing," she said kindly.

I nodded and made my way to the next office. As I turned to leave, the weight of the moment pressed down on me. The snow outside had begun to fall harder, blanketing the world in white. I stepped into the hallway, the door clicking shut be-hind me. For a long moment, I just stood there, staring at the swirling snow, feeling utterly alone.

***

"Hi there," the HR representative greeted me with a warm smile, her demeanor immediately putting me at ease. She re-minded me so much of Holly Flax from *The Office*—if Holly were about ten years younger. "I'm here to walk you through what's happening and answer any questions you have." She gestured to the chair across from her desk and said, "Please, have a seat. I know this is a lot to take in."

I sat down and nodded.

She continued, "I want you to know, this isn't personal. As a new nurse in your first year, you're on probation. The process we've used is designed to be non-adversarial. It's not about right or wrong—just a matter of procedure, really."

I looked at her, anxiety still swirling in my chest. "So... what does that mean for my license? Will anything be reported?"

She shook her head, reassuringly. "No. Losing a popularity contest is not grounds for reporting."

"And what if I apply somewhere else? Should I be worried about references?"

"No. HR will only confirm the dates you worked here. We won't say you were pushed out or anything like that—just that you left."

***

The paperwork given to me was impersonal and did not feel real. The NEC seemed to be on my side when I met them. Their official response was this:

*The NEC met to review Miles Smith, RN's performance during his probationary period. Miles attended the meeting with his union representative, Sarah, and provided both a written and verbal statement.*

*After reviewing all information, the committee recommends releasing Miles from employment. The decision is based on documented concerns about critical thinking, medication management, and patient safety. The committee also concluded that Miles did not fully recognize or understand his performance issues, even after his orientation was extended.*

*The committee noted that management had provided additional training and support throughout his orientation. Miles also reported concerns about unequal treatment and discrimination, and the president advised him of his option to contact the local Equal Employment Opportunity (EEO) office.*

The CEO of the hospital, Sandy, had her own document along with the NEC results. The NEC only recommended what to do. She had the authority to do something else or enact their recommendations. This was her response given to me:

*You were hired as a full-time nurse and placed on a one-year probationary period. You were informed that the NEC would review your performance and conduct during this period and make a recommendation about whether you should remain employed or be released. After completing this review, the NEC recommended—and I agree—that you be released during your probationary period.*

*HCO policy requires the organization to report licensed health care professionals to the appropriate state licensing boards if their clinical practice falls significantly below accepted standards and raises concerns about patient safety. If it is determined that your practice did not meet these standards, the organization will consider whether a report to the licensing board is necessary.*

*If you believe this action is the result of discrimination based on race, color, religion, sex, national origin, age, or disability, you may file a complaint with the EEO office within 45 calendar days. You must return all HCO property before receiving your final paycheck. Until the effective date of your release, you will remain in duty status and are expected to report to work as scheduled.*

*If you have questions about this action, you may contact Mr. Dipsitt in Human Resources at hrDipsitt@hco.org. The HCO also offers an Employee Help Program for individuals experiencing personal difficulties that may affect their performance,*

***

As I walked out to the parking lot, Monica was already waiting for me, engine running. I slid into the passenger seat. She looked over, her eyes searching my face.

"What happened?" she asked, her voice tense.

I shook my head, still in disbelief. "They let me go. After everything... they said it's a non-adversarial separation. I have two weeks left, and then I'm done."

Monica's jaw tightened. "Are you serious? After all the years you gave them? That's—" She stopped herself, then reached over and squeezed my hand. "That's not you, honey. This is their loss, not yours."

I stared out the window, the weight of it all pressing down. "I just... I wanted to retire here. I thought I was doing everything right."

She squeezed my hand tighter. "Listen to me. We're going to make the most of these next two weeks. God's got something better for you. Don't let them make you doubt yourself."

I managed a small smile. "You think so?"

She nodded. "Let's go have some fun. And when the right job comes along, you'll know it."

For the first time that day, I felt a flicker of hope. "Thanks, hon. I don't know what I'd do without you."

She winked. "Yeah, you *should* thank me."

That night, we attended our friend's wedding. We drank, laughed, and danced like no one was watching. Before midnight, as Monica slept, I opened my laptop and applied for three cool jobs that I wished I had had from the get-go. I got interviews and offers on all three within two weeks.

# PART II: A WARMER LIGHT

# 2

Later, the following February—a yellow call light rang through the silent corridor of a surgical trauma step-down unit in Wylde Town Falls's Large Teaching Hospital, *LTH*. I stepped up from my massive Phillips computer screen where I was getting ahead on charting and went to answer it. The unit was warm, and the white snowscape outside felt oddly comforting.

The patient was an elderly gentleman who spoke like he'd walked straight out of Gone with the Wind and looked like the type to wear a turtleneck under his blazer at a pretentious country club.

"Hello sir, how can I help you?" I asked.

"Well son, it appears that suppository you gave me for my lack of bowel motility has not worked," he said.

"Oh."

"I feel that my... my cheeks got a little too excited and squished too hard before it could properly migrate inward, and now it has been expulsed from my rectum and is cleft in twang. I have it here for your inspection and would like to request another suppository in its stead."

I looked at the bisected suppository in his hand, and I thanked God I was wearing gloves already. "You certainly did. I'll throw this away and get right on that, sir."

As I left to get another suppository from the Omnicell—a computerized, secure, machine where our drugs are kept and from which they are dispensed—I heard a man scream the kind of scream one screams likely when one was being murdered with an axe. Shelley, our newest nurse, had had another mishap.

We drew up heparin—a subcutaneously injected blood thinner used for clot prevention—using large-gauge blunt needles. Afterwards, we would discard the blunt needle in the disposable sharps container and replace it with a much smaller gauge one—usually around 25 to 26 gauge—that was less painful and much more humane to inject under the skin.

It was a somewhat painful stick, and it was followed by the burning heparin injected. The upside with a smaller gauge needle was that it had less tissue trauma than its larger counterparts. Shelley didn't exchange the blunt needle. It was like stabbing a man with a screwdriver.

This was not the first of her screw ups. The week prior, she had been tasked with giving an old lady a soap suds enema, which typically comes with a bag and hose. The enema hose has a cap—one that was supposed to be removed.

Shelley made sure to lubricate the tube before inserting it into the lady's rectum, but she forgot all about the cap on the end of the hose and lost it in the body. We were a teaching institution, and the resident physicians were especially eager to learn and do things. They went looking for the missing cap with a rectally inserted scope courtesy of our Gastrointestinal (GI) Service, and eventually, they found and removed it.

Shelley's first few weeks on the unit were anything but easy. She'd already had her share of mishaps, but each time, the team rallied around her with support and retraining rather than blame. It was clear Shelley was determined to learn, and everyone could see her potential. There was never any talk of Shelley facing an NEC.

One evening, as the shift settled into its usual rhythm, Shelley lingered by the medication cart, clutching a PCA kit and glancing nervously at the instructions. I noticed her hesitation and offered a gentle smile.

Shelley approached me, her voice barely above a whisper. "Hey, Miles... I know you're busy, but could you help me set up this PCA? I've read the instructions twice, but I'm still worried I'll mess something up."

I smiled reassuringly. "Of course, Shelley. Let's do it together. It's always better to ask than to guess."

Shelley handed me the PCA kit, her hands slightly trembling. "I just... I don't want to hurt anyone. I keep thinking about that heparin needle mistake last week."

"Hey, everyone makes mistakes when they're learning. What matters is that you care enough to double-check. That's what makes a good nurse." I walked Shelley through each step, explaining as I went. "See how the PCA module locks in? You want to make sure the tubing is primed before you connect it to the patient. Prime it using the pump, like this."

Shelley nodded, following along and asking questions. "So, after I program the dose, I need a second nurse to verify?"

"Exactly. I'll sign off with you to start. And if you ever feel unsure about anything, just ask. No judgment here."

Shelley smiled, visibly more relaxed. "Thanks, Miles. I really appreciate it. I wish I could be as calm as you."

"You will be. It just takes practice—and a little help from your friends."

Shelley laughed softly. "I hope one day I can help someone else like this."

"You absolutely will. That's how we all get better."

By the time we finished setting up the PCA, Shelley's shoulders had finally dropped from around her ears.

"Miles," she said, letting out a breath that sounded like relief wrapped in exhaustion, "thank you. Really."

"You're doing great. You'd be surprised how fast this stuff starts to click."

She gave a small, crooked smile. "I hope so. I feel like I'm asking a million questions."

"That's how you know you're going to be a good nurse."

When she walked away, I felt that familiar tug of responsibility—the same one I remembered from my own early days. I made a mental note to show her where we kept the subcutaneous injection needles and remind her to switch out the blunt needles after drawing up heparin. She'd get there. Sometimes all someone needs is for one person to believe in them.

***

In short order, this had become a wildly different time for me. I was now working in this incredible job with two of my best friends from nursing school taking care of surgical trauma patients. Trauma Drama blurred the line between step-down and ICU. I wasn't under stimulated at all.

I was shedding stress weight from nursing school and the hell I'd escaped. I was working out more, feeling good, and eating better. Two weeks after I was told I was leaving the Mountainton Medical Center, I started orientation to Trauma Drama. My life was turning around in such a positive way.

I had some of the sickest patients that I've ever had including gunshot wound victims, extended recovery after surgery patients, and postoperative Whipple surgeries. The latter of which had gone from being a dangerous death sentence of a surgery to a very routine dance of one with an extremely specific way in which these patients were cared for in their immediate recovery.

My orientation was supposed to be three weeks, but the Megs—three different nurses who all happened to be named Meg—had other ideas. After a few shifts with them, they pulled me aside at the nurses' station.

"Miles," the first Meg said, tapping her clipboard with a grin, "we've been comparing notes, and you don't need four weeks with us."

The second Meg nodded. "You're catching on fast."

"Really fast," the third added. "Marge is going to be thrilled."

They brought their notes to Marge, our nurse manager, and before I knew it, my orientation had been shortened to two weeks. I'll never forget that first day with the first Meg. As we walked into our first patient's room, she glanced over at me and said softly, almost like she didn't want to spook me, "I'm not here to scare you, test you, or trip you up. I'm here to teach you. We all are."

And just like that, I understood—for the first time—what a kind, sincere preceptor nurse was supposed to be. It felt like stepping into sunlight after months underground.

It was cool to see how someone could go from acutely ill to being on the mend. I had had sick patients with perforated bowels, patients needing to be coded or rapid responsed due to their acutely ill states, and I also was getting recognized for my work. LTH was incredible, and I loved working here. I must admit, however, that every nursing stereotype regarding working harder with a more horrific schedule for less pay was very present here. They made up for it in the culture though.

It seemed like I was getting thank you messages of recognition from patients and coworkers weekly. My coworkers were some of the nicest people I had ever met and some of the coolest, rockstar nurses. Every time I had anxiety about asking them for help with something or had a question, they were so happy, eager, and willing to help me.

I was grateful and said, "Thank you" every time, and they always answered with an easy, genuine "Of course!"—the kind of reply that told me they truly meant it. So, when Marge pulled me aside one morning and told me how well I was doing, that she wanted me to start training for charge nurse later that year, my jaw just about hit the floor. After everything I'd been through, hearing that felt like someone had opened a window in a room I didn't realize had gone dark.

***

The motley crew of characters that I got to work with were fun. Among my favorites was Cody. He was naturally energetic and happy. He was taller than me and had an entire sleeve of tattoos going down one arm. Despite his voracious energy, he had the calm demeanor of a surfer dude and no filter to his positive, explosive energy.

Every time we talked it was always "Hell yeah! Fuck yeah, man!" I do recall working many a night with him just laughing our asses off about anything, no matter how random. My favorite exploit of his happened when I was taking care of a

Baptist church youth minister who had come in for a bowel resection.

I had managed this man's pain well, which is to say I beat him at watching the clock and making sure he was medicated without having to hit his call light for it. He was constantly saying in his sweet timid voice, "Bless you, my son. You are amazing."

One night, I had to go in and increase his PCA dosage, per the doctor's order, because his pain was getting slightly more difficult to manage. A PCA is a patient-controlled analgesia drip, which means the patient is given a handheld button that they can press when they would like the self-administer a dose of intravenous pain medication. This medicine is locked in a special syringe-containing module attached to the Intravenous (IV) Pump with their other IV fluids, and it has a programmed lockout time and maximum dose they can self-administer to prevent overdosing.

To change the dosage at any time requires a special key that must be drawn out of the computerized medication dispenser to unlock the PCA and allow programming. Two nurses must sign off on it, and the key must be returned to the machine afterwards. This also requires a sign off on its return.

For this process on this night, Cody was my number two nurse. He energetically and helpfully barged in yelling, "Hell yeah, man, let's get this PCA INCREASED! Let's get shit done. Ah shit, the key's jammed! Got it. Okay, now let's really get it done." To say the least, the look on the youth pastor's face was PRICELESS. I absolutely love Cody, and I keep up with him.

***

Another interesting turn of events was when a well-meaning hippie couple brought in some homemade sweets to thank us for taking care of their loved one and give us a "de-stressor." I was too busy to partake, but when Marge came around, she looked in my eyes deeper than my true love. "Did you have any of the brownies in the break room, Miles?" she asked.

"There's brownies in the break room?" My hungry stomach growled hopefully. I was four and a half hours into the shift without a single morsel of nourishment, and I was excited at the thought of a brownie.

"Well not anymore. This patient's family brought in brownies for you guys that were tainted. We are sending three of your co-workers and a resident to the ED. They had some, and now they're having bad reactions!"

"What kind of bad reactions?"

"They're disoriented. Panicked. The resident has stiffened her body out like a board, and she's all tensed up, rigid, and not talking! It's really bad! She might be seizing or maybe it's a stroke!"

Too bad I didn't get a bite of those brownies, I thought.

"Anyway," Marge continued, "I need you to take on two more patients. I know you're busy, but I'm counting on you, because we're so short staffed in the whole hospital."

I wanted to cry at the thought of taking more patients but given how great I was being treated in contrast to the Mountainton Medical Center, I wasn't going to complain. Marge had been in the Army, and we had bonded over our shared veteran status and work ethic. I was very loyal to her and would have done anything for her as one of her nurses.

No bullshit here—on the day my co-workers were drugged, I got my ass **kicked**. I was sprinting in and out of rooms, grabbing bites of lunch like a raccoon stealing food between dumpster dives, and I was so slammed I couldn't even make it to the bathroom when nature demanded its moment. I cut off my underwear with trauma shears and finished the shift commando. The answer, my friend, is blowing in the wind—and it was as cold as a well-digger's ass in Idaho during Mountainton's winter, FYI. Monica still hasn't let me live that one down.

As hellacious as that day was, I can say I made it through, and I did that in an ocean of camaraderie with some of the best nurses I've worked with. The brownies were laced with LSD. That explained why three smart nurses and one doctor couldn't find their way out of a room with one door.

# 3

I was still getting texts from Joanie, my nursing scholarship mentor at Mountainton Medical Center. Every scholarship recipient was paired with a mentor to help guide them into nursing practice, but Joanie had been kept at arm's length during my time on TU. When she finally realized what was happening, she told me she wished she'd stepped in sooner.

The texts were usually one of two types: *Are you okay?* or *Hey, checking in!*

At first, I got these twice a week. When they slowed down, I thought that chapter had finally closed. Joanie never let me go after the hospital did.

Joanie was a lifelong nurse who had done nearly everything one could do in the profession. She had her master's degree in healthcare leadership. With the current leadership in place, she wasn't allowed to hold positions that would use her degree due to her being more qualified than they. Insane, I know, but she would one day have her due when that leadership regime fell.

I know for a while she was scared that I was going to harm myself. For a while, the texts stopped, but that April, she contacted me. "Hey, I have some news," she said.

"What's up?" I thought aloud.

"Well," she said, and I could hear the weight she'd been carrying in her voice, "I had to report what they did to you to national IICO Headquarters. Technically..." She hesitated, almost wincing. "Technically, you're in breach of your scholarship contract because you got let go."

My stomach dropped. "What?" was all I could manage.

Joanie spoke, her tone soft but urgent, like she was trying to steady me from across the distance between us. "Listen to me," she said. "You won't pay a dime of that money back. Not one cent. You didn't do anything wrong. What they did to you was unacceptable—everyone can see it but them."

She let out a slow breath, the kind you release when you've already fought battles on someone else's behalf. "But…" Her voice softened with something like regret. "There is a catch, though."

The way she said it told me the next part would hurt. And for the first time in months, I felt someone standing between me and the fallout, instead of someone pushing me toward it.

"I'm listening," I said.

And I don't like where this could be going, I thought.

"National is sympathetic to your case, and they want you to officially report to them what happened. You must petition for a scholarship waiver of financial liability. Likely, they are going to try to push for you to go back to work for the HCO."

I couldn't believe it, and honestly, I kept telling myself there was no way that would ever happen. I couldn't imagine the hospital ever allowing it. Josey—my former nurse manager—was a darling to the executive team. The executives loved her, practically fawned over her. People like that don't get questioned; they get protected.

She was being groomed to climb the promotion ladder. Her performance was abysmal in the eyes of her employees, and she yielded many EEO complaints that fell on deaf ears.

She was being groomed by Kelly, the senior nurse officer who gave me a speech akin to George Clooney's in the beginning of the movie Up in the Air when letting me go.

Kelly was a poor ICU nurse but an excellent corporate climber. She also used the hospital's scholarship money for her degree. She had had no children, but Josey was like her daughter. She trained her well in the art of causing harm to others—her employees. There existed a common belief amongst Kelly and her posse of superiors and acolytes—to make yourself look awesome, make another look awful.

Kelly was the person who introduced to her superior, the patient services manager, that cuts to different programs within the hospital should be made to save money. The cuts proposed included funding for the scholarships that earned her and me our respective degrees and many different staffing positions to the inpatient nursing pool, which was already understaffed. She also did questionable iron fist policies such as counting sick calls as no call, no show and denying vacation requests to see if the employee would react or fight back.

The patient services manager, Mr. Farley, was rigid, punitive, and beloved by upper leadership. Outside of work, he was a husband, a father, a coach, and a devoted member of his charismatic church in town. He spoke with a thick Southern accent and carried himself with the kind of rigid righteousness that made every minor infraction feel like a personal insult to him. His leadership style was straight out of *Sinners in the Hands of an Angry God*—reactive, punishing, and always tipped to the extreme.

I used to think that if he ever made peace with himself, maybe he would've been more relaxed, more human. But that never happened. Instead, he clung tightly to appearances, to rules, to whatever kept him untouchable in the eyes of the executive team. And it worked. Farley was a darling of upper leadership—a groomed successor, practically hand-picked to take over when the CEO retired.

Sandy, the CEO in question, was the one who rubber-stamped my dismissal without a second thought. It still struck me as strange that she never met with me—not once. She was known for sitting down with nurses who were in trouble or facing discipline, giving them a second chance instead of sending them out the door. That was her thing. She liked to hear their side of it.

I never met her, and I never met Mr. Farley either. Because of that, Joanie's insistence that I might go back to work for the Mountainton Medical Center, as I assumed, felt almost impossible to believe. Far-fetched didn't even begin to cover it.

"What are the chances they just let me move on?" It came out quieter than I meant it to—half hope, half dread.

I heard Joanie exhale slowly on the other end of the line, the kind of breath someone takes when they're about to say something they wish they didn't have to. "I don't know," she said gently. "I mean... that is a possibility."

The way she said it—soft, hesitant—told me she wanted to protect me, but even she didn't fully believe the odds were in my favor. And somehow, that scared me more than the words themselves.

She went on, her voice weighted with equal parts urgency and regret. "I hope you petition them for that. You need to. And you need to write to the head of the organization and the head of the scholarship section and tell them exactly what happened to you. It's the only shot you have at getting them to help you—or getting off the obligatory hook."

She paused, and I could almost hear her debating how honest to be before she continued. "But Miles... I also think there's a lot of good you could do for this organization if you came back. And I think they're going to want you to do that instead of just letting you walk away free and clear."

Another small pause—soft, reluctant, but hopeful. "This could work in your favor," she said, though even through the phone I could feel the heaviness behind those words. It wasn't a promise. It was a warning wrapped in compassion, and we both knew it.

"This could work in your favor" had become a loaded phrase. Obviously, it wasn't right when Kelly said so, given this current situation. I didn't see how it could be any truer at this juncture.

"Well, as much as I always wanted to work there, I can't. How can I with such an iron curtain that put me out in the first place?" I surmised.

She replied, "Well... you'd have to work at one of the other hospitals for the organization—in another state."

I blinked, stunned. "Another state? Seriously?"

Joanie didn't hesitate. "I know it's a lot. Believe me, I do." Her voice softened, the kind of gentle tone someone uses when they wish they could shield you from what they're about to say. "But if you want the scholarship issue resolved, that's the route they're going to push for. And you'd be good there, Miles. You really would."

I let out a shaky breath. "But... I finally found a place I fit. I'm learning. I'm healing. I don't want to start over again. Not like this."

"I understand," she said quietly. "And I'm not saying it's fair, because it isn't. But you have people rooting for you at the national level—people who actually want to help you. If going to another state is what gets you free of what Mountainton did to you... then we need to consider it." Her words hung there—heavy, unwelcome, but spoken with love.

I hesitated, then added quietly, "I don't want to work with shitty people again, Joanie. I barely survived it the first time."

Joanie listened, and then she told me, "The organization is not just the Mountainton Medical Center, Miles. It's not just That Unit. There are good people in it. You know that we're not all shitty."

I took a breath and said, "I know."

"Good. So, tell your story," Joanie said. "They cannot get away with this. Light them up!"

***

I sat down at my computer with a glass of wine, and I metaphorically opened the wounds. This type of bleeding hurt, and it hurt a whole hell of a lot. I refilled the wine more times than I would like to admit when I wrote the emails to the heads of the organization and the scholarship section. None of it was easy to share.

I sat there for a long time before I wrote it.

The email to the head of the organization stared back at me, blank, waiting.

When I finally started typing, I told him everything—how I went from a combat veteran to a nurse, and what had happened on That Unit. I explained how management shut me out every time I tried to be heard, how my scholarship—and my entire career—was now on the line because of it

I told him how it felt. Unjust. Isolating. Like I was already being written off before anyone listened.

*I'm not asking for sympathy,* I wrote. *I'm asking to be heard.*

I attached everything I had—evidence, character references, a journaled timeline of events.

And then I sent it.

Hoping it would be enough. Hoping someone, somewhere, would finally listen.

I wrote a second email—this one to the head of the scholarship program.

This one had a different weight to it.

This one wasn't just about being heard. It was about what I owed—and what I might lose.

I formally requested a waiver for my service and repayment obligations under the HCO scholarship program.

As I wrote it, I tried to keep my tone measured. Professional. Controlled.

But underneath that, everything was unraveling.

*My separation from the organization was not voluntary,* I wrote. *I was placed on a unit where I was not wanted, subjected to false accusations, and ultimately released during my probationary period despite my efforts to succeed.*

I told them who I was—my background as a veteran, my work in healthcare, what I had accomplished in nursing school, and why I still believed in the work.

I told them I hadn't given up—I had been forced out.

*I remained willing to serve and continue within the organization in another capacity,* I wrote.

And I meant it.

I told them that maybe, under different circumstances, I would come back and fulfill what I had committed to.

Then I sent it.

Their response came back polite. Clean. Distant.

An apology. Acknowledgment. A promise that my case would be reviewed.

Nothing more.

It didn't bring closure.

But it was a turning point.

I had said everything I needed to say—to the people who had the power to change it.

At the bottom of both emails, I left them with a quote:

*"A lie doesn't become truth, wrong doesn't become right, and evil doesn't become good, just because it's accepted by a majority."*

— Booker T. Washington

4

During this time, one of the most meaningful things that happened was the outpouring of support I received from friends—RTs and nurses I'd worked with, my nursing instructors, and even colleagues from That Unit who spoke up in direct contradiction to the picture Josey and her gang were trying to paint of me. Their letters carried weight. Their words carried me. The first came from a preceptor on That Unit.

*To Whom It May Concern.*

*I am writing to speak of the qualities of Miles, whom I worked with for four months on a medical-surgical ward at Mountainton Medical Center. I have worked more closely with Miles, as one of his preceptors in the field of nursing, for a period of three weeks.*

*I have had the chance to get to know Miles, and I say with no doubt that you are dealing with a person of exceptionally good moral character. Miles works with integrity, is hardworking, and dedicated to patient care.*

*Throughout the three weeks of nurse training Miles was consistent in his work ethic. He was eager to learn by assessing the patient care setting and asking well thought out questions. Miles interacted with patients in a sincere, caring manner. He made use of various research tools available to better understand the patient's condition, disease process, medications he administered, and the proper patient education needed at dis-*

*charge. Miles will continue to make himself aware of patient needs, meet those needs, and succeed in the field of nursing.*

*I have also noticed Miles is up for anything and never complains about the work set before him. I look forward to working with him in the coming months and years. In this hospital setting, nursing and patient care require teamwork. I believe Miles will always function as a formidable team player.*

*Please contact me if you would like me to answer any questions or give you specific examples.*

*Sincerely,*

*Yogi, RN*

***

This was from a nursing school preceptor.

*My name is Kim. I am an RN on Step-Down at Mountainton Medical Center. I have known Miles for approximately five years. I worked with Miles for several years in his role as respiratory therapist, prior to his entry into nursing school at Awesome University. I served as clinical scholar to students from Awesome University during their second clinical in the nursing program. Miles was among these students.*

*Miles excelled during this rotation and received consistently positive feedback. He arrived prepared for each clinical day, and his care plans were well written. At every turn, Miles provided safe, ethical, and competent care. Miles possesses a curious and inquisitive mind and if there was anything he was unsure of, he made a point to research it or ask for help.*

*He had the confidence to seek out new experiences and knowledge and had the utmost integrity in his nursing care. He was also able to establish rapport with every patient he worked with.*

*I recall many times that Miles showed excellent critical thinking when trying to solve problems. I also recall a code blue situation when Miles stepped up to the front of the room and offered his help. I was so impressed by his initiative, willingness to help, and his calm and sure presence during chaos.*

*Of all the students in his group, Miles was the most enthusiastic and excited to become a nurse. He is the type of nurse that I look forward to working alongside and with whom I know I can trust to do his absolute best. In Miles's role as new nurse, he deserves to be supported and championed as he finds his way in this crazy profession that we all have chosen.*

*He not only served his country but also wishes to dedicate his life to serving by providing excellent nursing care. He deserves our respect and patience as he continues in this profession. I speak as a member of the nursing profession when I say that Miles will make nursing and the hospital proud if we stand beside him and support him to be his very best.*

*Sincerely yours,*

*Kim, RN*

***

Perhaps what was most impactful was a letter my dad sent.

*To Whom It May Concern:*

*It is my understanding that Miles is separated from the HCO's hospital in Mountainton, CO, where he was previously employed, due to alleged performance deficiencies and misconduct, after serving the HCO for 5 years. These alleged deficiencies were said to have occurred during a brief time with a preceptor.*

*The purpose of this letter is to shed light on the character traits of my son, as seen over his entire lifetime as follows:*

At age 11, he began part-time work and was praised early for his strong work ethic.

At age 17, anxious to serve his country, he joined the US Army Reserve and trained in the Military Police Battalion in Bigtown, MS.

He graduated with honors from high school in Riverwood, MS the summer prior to his senior year by taking extra courses periodically. Although they did not normally allow a student to graduate early, an exception was made for Miles when he told his principal, "I want to serve my country."

At age 18, following high school graduation, Miles transferred to full-time US Army and trained at Ft Benning, GA. While there, he suffered a high ankle sprain, and his graduation was delayed. He toughed out the sprain, completed the training, and graduated.

He completed infantry and air assault training before serving two combat tours in Iraq.

Miles served in the Iraqi Conflict for approximately 12 months made up of 2 combat tours of approximately 6 months each. While serving in Iraq, he received the following honors:

(see attachments)

1) The Army Commendation Medal

2) Certificate of Achievement for Outstanding Performance including 250 route clearances, 90 successful raids, sniper mission participation, providing aid to an injured Iraqi citizen, and providing security during a Special Forces Mission critical to mission success.

3) The Army Achievement Medal for Meritorious Achievement as the Soldier of the Month where the Company Com-

*mander and the Battalion Commander highly commended him.*

*4) US Army Combat Infantry Badge*

*Miles returned to Ft Benning, Georgia and received an Honorable Discharge from the US Army just in time to begin college.*

*After the Army, Miles completed his education in respiratory care and nursing, earning multiple academic honors.*

*During orientation, Miles reported harassment, false accusations, and being told veterans belonged in hospital beds, not at the bedside.*

*The allegations that are made toward Miles and which resulted in a Nursing Evaluation Committee hearing and his separation from the hospital, are, simply put, contrary to the Miles that I know and have known for his entire life.*

*Granted, Miles is my son and for that reason alone, I love him dearly. However, I also know him as a person and as a man. Miles is a brilliant young man, a Combat Infantry Badged Disabled Veteran, a US patriot, an American hero, and one who has received honors in high school, during time of active-duty service in the US Army, in junior college, and in senior college. We need more people like him in this profession.*

*It is truly unbelievable and a travesty that the HCO, through its management team, has chosen to separate from an individual who has the qualities that Miles has. It is especially alarming when he has kept a clean record of service with the Mountainton Medical Center for the pasts 5 years. It is especially difficult to swallow since he is a decorated disabled veteran who is being separated by a small group of non-veterans who could not understand the commitment that our veterans make to our country nor the trails that they traveled for our free-dom.*

*Finally, it is my understanding that Miles has asked that he be relieved of any financial responsibility to the HCO for the HCO scholarship that he was awarded and by which he received his BSN RN while receiving the Excellence in Nursing Award also. Surely, it would add insult to injury to ask him to reimburse the HCO since the HCO, through its managers, is not allowing him to continue work there and honor his commitment to do so in return for the scholarship.*

*It is a sad day when an entity cannot or will not do the right thing because it must or believes that it must protect its reputation and/or its managers who have made a horrendous mistake and have misjudged one of America's best. A father must wonder why.*

*Respectfully,*
*Father of Miles, BSN, RN, RRT*

***

Those were only some of the letters of support I received and gave along with my evidence. In all, 32 people spoke up for me. They all wrote letters for me, and they put their names and reputation on the line to vouch for mine.

Looking back, the emails were too much. Trauma isn't pretty.

I sent these letters along with my other evidence to both the heads of the organization and the scholarship section. Dad's letter carried a lot of impact. I never thought I had made him proud, but after reading his letter, I knew I did. Reading the letters overwhelmed me.

Things carried on as usual on Trauma Drama. I immersed myself into the ocean of camaraderie and swam. Every interaction with every nurse, every friend with whom I now worked, felt so urgent, so precious, so finite.

I didn't know what to expect from the national HCO. I assumed the responses were lip service. I hoped and waited in anticipation for a waiver to be granted relieving me of my scholarship obligation. I heard nothing but silence from them for the next month and a half.

Then, I got a phone call...

# 5

I got the call in late May. His voice was soft and friendly—the kind you'd expect from an older, wiser man from Texas. "Hey, howya doin,' son. My name's Earl. I've read and heard a whole lot about you. Whole lot of stuff goin' on behind the scenes on account of you. I understand they done ya pretty dirty in Mountainton.".

He cut straight to business. It was refreshing.

"They were pretty awful," I told him.

He went on, "Well, the scholarship section wants me to work with you and git you back workin' with the organization."

It was a lot to take in. For a moment I just sat silent, trying to process the words. "How... how is that even possible after everything that happened?" I finally asked.

Earl chuckled with that easy Southern calm of his, the kind that made you feel like life couldn't possibly be as bad as it seemed. "Son, you'd be surprised what can happen when the right folks finally read the truth. You ain't the first person to get done dirty by a hospital in this organization, but you *are* one of the few I've seen who had damn near half the town writin' letters on his behalf."

He gave a low whistle. "They noticed."

His words didn't settle me. "I don't understand how they'd take me back," I said. "They tossed me out like trash."

I imagined Earl shook his head. "Mountainton tossed ya out; Big HCO didn't." That hit me harder than I expected.

He kept talking like he had all day, "They want me to help you get planted somewhere new. Clean slate. Different hospital, different leadership, different folks who ain't gunnin' for ya. You give 'em what they're askin' for, and they'll give you a way back in."

He paused, awaiting my reaction. "You did nothin' wrong, Miles. Folks higher up know that now. That's why I'm here."

"Then... why can't they just let me off the hook?" I asked. "Why can't they just let me move on with my life and be done with all this?"

Earl gave a slow sigh, the sympathetic kind. "Son, I wish it worked like that. I truly do. But big organizations? They move like freight trains—slow to turn, even slower to stop. You're tied up in scholarship money, policy, paperwork, politics... and folks up top don't wanna set a precedent they gotta answer for later."

"Shit," I said barely audible, and I let out a long sigh.

He continued, "They ain't tryin' to punish you anymore. They're tryin' to fix what was done to ya—but they can't do that by just wavin' a wand and lettin' you go."

I swallowed hard. "So, what happens now?"

"Let me ask you somethin', Miles," he said. "You ever thought about Texas?"

"Texas? What about it?"

Earl let out a slow "mm-hmm" the way old sergeants do when they're about to hand you a truth you're not sure you want. "Son, Big HCO's got hospitals all over. Some good, some bad, some downright miraculous. And down in Texas... well, let's just say leaderships got a whole different flavor. Folks there ain't carryin' grudges from Mountainton. They don't know Josey, don't know Farley, don't know any of that mess. They'd just know *you*."

I rubbed my forehead. "Earl... I just got out of hell. I finally found a place I fit. And now they want me to start all over? Somewhere completely different?"

He replied, not unkindly, "Yep. That's about the size of it."

"And this is the only way? There's really no option where they just let me walk away and move on with my life?"

"Miles, if it were up to me, I'd sign the papers myself and tell ya to go fishin' for the rest of your life. But big organizations don't do simple. They want their boxes checked, their strings tied, their debts settled in whatever damn way their rulebook says makes sense."

I sighed, leaning back. "I just... I don't want another Mountainton. I don't want to go through that again."

I could hear him giving whatever table or desk he was at a firm tap with his fingers. "And you won't. 'Cause I ain't gonna let you land in another Mountainton. You hear me? I ain't sendin' you into the lion's den. I'm sendin' you somewhere folks'll give you a fair shake."

I swallowed, his words settling heavier than I expected.

"Now, let me ask you somethin' else, Miles," he went on, lowering his voice. "You ever had real Texas barbecue?"

Despite myself, I almost laughed. "Can't say that I have."

"Well, hell," he said, slapping his desk, "then that's your sign right there. Maybe the good Lord's tellin' ya it's time to come on down and see what all the fuss is about."

I shook my head, but I was smiling now too. "You really think this could work out?"

Earl spoke with that quiet military confidence. "Son, I ain't in the business of blowin' smoke. If I tell ya you can land on your feet down there, it's 'cause I've seen enough to know you can. Let me help you get there."

***

Earl insisted it wouldn't feel real unless Monica heard it from him. "She ain't gonna believe a word of this unless she hears it from the horse's mouth," he'd said, and he wasn't wrong. So, we booked the flights.

A week later, Monica and I were sitting side-by-side on a plane headed to Super-Hot City, Texas. She held my hand the entire ascent, her thumb tracing circles over my knuckles the way she did whenever I was trying too hard to pretend I wasn't anxious.

"You okay?" she asked softly.

I nodded, but it was the kind of nod that lied by omission. "Yeah. Just... can't believe we're doing this."

She rested her head on my shoulder. "I know. But if this is what gets us free, we'll figure it out. Together, baby."

Her faith in me had always felt like some kind of undeserved magic.

The flight wasn't long, but every mile felt like it carried a piece of the life we'd built in Colorado. I stared out the window, trying to picture myself starting over again. New hospital. New unit. New people. Same organization that had just chewed me up and spit me out.

"Hey," Monica whispered, nudging my arm gently. "You're not alone in this."

I exhaled and squeezed her hand. "I know. I'm just... scared. I don't want another Mountainton. I don't want to walk into a new place already looking over my shoulder."

"And maybe you won't have to," she said. "Maybe this is the part where things turn around."

I wanted to believe her.

When the plane descended, heat hit us the second the doors opened—Texas heat, thick and unapologetic. It felt like stepping into another world.

After we'd left our things in our hotel room, we met Earl himself at the Super-Hot City Medical Center. He was leaning casually against a railing like he'd been waiting all morning just to greet us. He raised a hand and hollered, "Hey! Y'all must be the Smiths!" before breaking into a wide grin. His accent alone convinced Monica he was real.

She looked at me like, *okay, maybe this really is happening.*

Earl was tall, friendly, and carried himself with easy authority. His starched suit and tie reflected this as well, though in the Texas heat, he had discarded his jacket into his giant and mighty Dodge Ram Super Duty Truck.

Earl had been in the Air Force, which he was sure to remind me. "We shit in the Marriott, not in the woods," he said to explain the difference between Army and Air Force life. He wasn't wrong. In the state I had been in, I had to appreciate how that joke made me genuinely laugh for the first time since Joanie foreshadowed dealing with the HCO again.

Earl greeted Monica first. "Ma'am," he said respectfully, shaking her hand with both of his. "I'm Earl—the one tryin' to help your husband out of that mess y'all been trapped in."

Monica blinked, taken aback by his warmth, then smiled. "Thank you. Really."

"Don't thank me yet," Earl said, chuckling. "Come on. Let me show y'all the hospital. And after that, we're gettin' barbecue. Real barbecue."

Monica's eyebrows lifted. "Real enough to make me forgive this heat?"

Earl laughed so loud a few people turned their heads. "Honey, by the time we're done, you're gonna forget Colorado even exists."

I wasn't sure about that—but for the first time in months, something in my chest loosened. Maybe it was the absurd heat. Maybe it was Earl. Maybe it was just the feeling of forward motion.

But whatever it was, I followed him.

The Super-Hot City Medical Center moved fast, and they didn't mess around. I interviewed with three units before lunch, Earl escorting me to each. Each person was nicer than the next. At lunch, Earl introduced us to Texas barbecue, and I thought my stomach was going to explode.

Before our flight back from Texas, Earl pulled me aside. "Listen," he said, his voice low but earnest, "I want you to give me everything you've got—all your documentation, anything they used against you. I need your full story so I can give my people the real picture."

For a moment, I hesitated, and he caught my eye. "I mean it. I want to hear it all, and I want to help. I care about what happened to you." For the first time in a long while, I believed him.

I gave him everything. My written response to the NEC and the timeline of events had been my chance to tell my side of the story to the NEC. I had written it while I was exiled in that office building at the replacement hospital and sitting in that cubicle in an empty office area.

Before meeting with the NEC, I sent them a comprehensive letter outlining my journey from Army veteran to nurse, my dedication to patient care, and the challenges I faced during orientation. In the letter, I described the bullying and false accusations I endured, my repeated efforts to seek help and improve, and the emotional toll these experiences took on my health and confidence.

I emphasized my commitment to safe practice, my willingness to learn, and my desire for a fair chance to continue my career. I provided evidence of my positive performance in earlier roles, character references from colleagues and mentors, and a detailed timeline of events to support my case.

Writing both was both painful and cathartic—a final attempt to share my truth and ask for understanding. I hoped the committee would see beyond the negative reports and recognize my integrity, resilience, and potential as a nurse. The NEC's response would decide my future, and I waited anxiously for their decision.

# PART III: THE DEN OF MISERY

6

Months before that October day at HR, I was already inside what I came to call the Den of Misery.

The people in this timeline are the ones most central to what happened. What follows is limited to what I personally witnessed. I've tried to be honest, knowing I can't see everything that happened outside my view.

I gave the NEC, the national HCO leaders, and Earl my honest account, without omission or embellishment. I gave the complete truth, as I experienced it. I shared these memories to provide a clear timeline of events from my perspective.

***

*Week One*

I stepped onto That Unit and smoothed the front of my new scrubs, trying to steady my nerves. The place showed its age—dingy linoleum, sagging tiles, buzzing fixtures, that faint musty undertone that never fully goes away. The new hospital couldn't come soon enough.

I spotted a young woman standing at the nurses' station, her posture straight, her hair pulled back with precision. She was younger than I expected for a manager, her eyes sharp. She glanced up, her smile polite but not quite reaching her eyes.

"You must be Miles," she said, her voice soft but businesslike.

"Yes, ma'am. First day," I replied, offering a hopeful smile.

She approached me and extended her hand. "I'm Josey, the nurse manager here. Welcome."

I shook her hand, noting the apathy in the firmness of her grip and the way she sized me up in a single glance. There was a pause—just long enough for me to sense something off.

Josey's smile faded as she looked me over. "I'll be honest, we weren't expecting you. We usually have a say in who joins this unit, and we had someone else in mind."

"I'm grateful for the opportunity. I'm here to learn and work hard."

She nodded, but her expression didn't soften. "You'll be starting orientation with Sassy; she's in the nurse's lounge. She'll show you the ropes. If you have questions, ask her or the charge nurse. We run a tight ship. Patient safety is our top priority."

I nodded, trying to hide my disappointment. I'd hoped for a warmer welcome, maybe a little encouragement. Instead, I felt like an outsider before I'd even begun.

Josey glanced at her watch. "I have a meeting to get to. Good luck, Miles."

With that, she turned and walked away, her heels clicking briskly down the hallway. I stood for a moment, letting the reality settle in. I took a deep breath, squared my shoulders, and headed toward the nurses' lounge to find Sassy—determined to make the best of a difficult first impression.

As I walked down the hall, the scent of antiseptic and the low hum of voices filled the air. I clutched my orientation folder a little tighter. The badge clipped to my scrubs felt heavier than usual.

A woman with sharp features and thin-framed glasses approached, her expression neutral but not unfriendly. She wore a badge that read, "Dakota, Assistant Nurse Manager."

"You must be Miles," Dakota said, extending a hand. Her grip was firm, her gaze steady. "Welcome. We're glad you're here."

"Thank you," I replied, managing a nervous smile.

Dakota gestured down the hallway. "Let me introduce you to a couple of folks before you get started."

We walked a short distance to where a petite woman with curly hair was reviewing a stack of papers at a workstation. Dakota tapped her gently on the shoulder.

"Amélie, this is Miles—our new grad nurse."

Amélie looked up, her face brightening. "Hi, Miles! Welcome aboard. I'm the nurse educator for the unit. If you need anything about equipment or procedures, I'm your go-to."

"Thank you, Amélie. I appreciate it."

Dakota nodded approvingly. "All right, let's get you to your preceptor."

We continued down the corridor, passing busy nurses and the steady beep of monitors. In the nurses' lounge, a woman with vibrant, purple hair and a quick smile was chatting with another nurse.

"Sassy," Dakota called, "this is Miles. He's starting orientation with you."

Sassy turned, her eyes sparkling with energy. "Hey, Miles! Ready to jump in?"

I grinned. "Absolutely. Looking forward to learning from you."

Dakota gave me a reassuring nod. "You're in good hands."

As she walked away, Sassy nudged my shoulder, "Don't let the Volturi scare you."

I laughed. "*Twilight*?"

"Exactly."

As Sassy began showing me around the unit, I glanced back to see Dakota and Amélie watching, both giving a small, encouraging wave.

I began my orientation under Sassy's preception. She was friendly, welcoming, and possessed a quick wit. I was excited to begin orientation, and I enjoyed working with her. We focused on patient assessments, charting, and medication administration, establishing a solid foundation for my transition into the unit.


## Week Two

Orientation continued under Sassy's guidance. During this time, we developed rapport, I became more familiar with the unit, and I started learning the processes for admitting and discharging patients. Sassy provided a positive first review to Josey and Dakota, noting several strengths and areas for improvement: *Charting: more descriptive, improving fast. Patient rapport: excellent. Load: managing four patients. Time management: improving. Confidence with MDs: keep building it.*


## Week Three

Orientation continued with Sassy. One afternoon, I approached her, holding the supplies for a new PCA setup.

"Can you walk me through priming the PCA syringe tubing with the pump again?"

"Sure," Sassy said. "Watch closely."

Later that shift, I asked again where the prime option lived in the menu.

Her tone sharpened. "I already showed you—twice. You need to start remembering."

She glanced at the syringe. "You almost hooked up un-primed tubing to a patient. That's dangerous."

"I didn't. I was double-checking before connecting any-thing."


### Week Four

Other orientees and I worked in the skills lab with Amélie, who taught us how to work various medical equipment and checked off our competencies. Much of the week consisted of PowerPoint presentations, but a highlight was practicing blood glucose checks on each other and learning to use the glucose monitors.

Tom, the most experienced new hire with a mischievous grin, rolled a glucose lancet between his thumb and index fin-ger. He glanced over at me—sizing up my nerves.

"You ready to find out if those donuts you demolished ear-lier are coming back to haunt you?" Tom teased, holding up the fresh lancet.

I tried to laugh it off, rubbing my fingertip. "Hey, I only had one... maybe two. Just go easy on me, okay?"

Tom grinned wider. "No promises, rookie. The first stick is always the deepest. Brace yourself!" He dramatically poised the lancet, pausing just long enough to make me flinch.

"Just get it over with!" I squeezed my eyes shut.

With a quick click, Tom did the fingerstick, then showed me the reading on the glucometer afterwards. "See? Survived and not diabetic. Now you can officially call yourself a nurse."

I shook my head, grinning despite myself. "It's going to be a long career."

Tom winked. "You'll get used to it."

## *Week Five*

The fluorescent lights intermittently blinked overhead as I finished charting, the steady rhythm of the unit broken only by the occasional call bell ringing. Sassy leaned against the counter, her now vibrant, red hair pulled back, eyes shadowed by fatigue and something deeper.

She glanced at me, then sighed, her voice low. "You ever feel like management just doesn't get it?" she asked.

I nodded. "It's tough."

She exhaled. "I vented to Dakota—she was my roommate before she became assistant manager. She went straight to Josey. Now Josey's furious and denied my time off."

"That rough," I said carefully.

After that, something shifted. Sassy's warmth cooled. When I asked questions, her answers got curt, and each shift felt heavier.

*Week Six*

Sassy approached me with a smile. "Hey, I wanted to talk to you about your charting," she said.

"Sure, what's up?" I replied, curious.

"Your charting could read less like an RT's and more like an RN's. Paint the picture."

"Can you give me some examples?"

"Of course. Take a look at my charting and compare it with some of the other nurses'. It might help you improve your documentation."

I agreed and spent some time reviewing the charts. Later, Sassy came back to check on my progress.

"How's it going?" she asked.

"I've been working on it. I think I'm getting the hang of it. Check out this note."

Sassy glanced over my note and nodded. "That's more like it."


*Week Seven*

During a busy shift, as I approached Sassy with equipment in hand for drawing blood cultures, I tried to keep my voice upbeat. "Can you talk me through blood cultures again? Just the bottle order."

She barely looked up. "We've already gone over that. You should know it by now."

"I just want to be sure—"

"I don't have time to repeat myself all shift. Figure it out."

Around noon, she handed me my second performance review—some fair feedback, and some claims that didn't match reality—*held back of hand to patient's forehead to tell if he had a fever, almost bolused a patient with an IV line full of air.*

Later that day, I was called into a meeting with Josey and Amélie. I told them plainly, "I didn't do the things she's describing. I'm still learning, like any new graduate nurse. But it feels like her personal frustrations are bleeding into my training."

Josey's decision was quick. "We've decided you'll orient with Amélie for one day, while Sassy is on vacation, and then with Yogi for the remainder of your day shift orientation."

***

Josey followed with an email:

*Hi Miles,*

*Your patient rapport is strong, and your documentation is improving. Please focus now on critical thinking in urgent moments and clarifying medications. You will work one day with Amélie, then transition to Yogi and submit a daily evaluation after each shift.*

*Remember, every shift is a new start—keep asking questions.*

*Best,*

*Josey*

# 7

Week Eight I worked a twelve-hour shift with Amélie. She took the more critical patient; I managed three less-critical patients. The day went smoothly, and Amélie's feedback indicated I was progressing.

After this shift, management confirmed I'd transition to Yogi. He would complete a daily preceptor evaluation, and I was required to submit a self-reflection after each shift. I wasn't given copies for my records, and I didn't receive written feedback or "corrections" until the NEC evidence packet.

***

Working with Yogi was a positive experience from day one. He greeted me with calm humor— "Ready for another day in paradise?"—and then did what good preceptors do: taught. He gave me an alphabetized medication list he'd made when he was new. "No shame in looking things up," he said. "Better to be safe than sorry." By the end of the shift, for the first time in weeks, I felt hopeful again

As the shifts unfolded, I found myself relaxing. Yogi's calm presence and dry wit made the chaos of the floor feel manageable. When I hesitated with a procedure, Yogi stepped in—not to take over, but to guide.

"Remember, Miles," Yogi said as we wrapped up a busy hour, "there's a thousand ways to do this job. You'll find your own. Ask questions, learn from everyone, and you'll be just fine."

Amélie's feedback was as follows: *good flow, good report, good documentation; doing well with three patients—move to four soon.*

Yogi's feedback was: *managed five patients; excellent time use (charting/meds/assessments); explained med purpose/side effects/doses; thorough handoff report; strong grasp of condition/needs; effective teaching; keep communicating with charge/CNAs/unit secretary.* "Nice work, Miles."

**Week Nine**

Orientation continued with Yogi. He reinforced skills I hadn't done recently (nasogastric tube insertions, wound care) and taught ostomy changes. His feedback: *great time use, strong medication understanding, good charting, outstanding patient communication; tasks and charting completed on time.*

**Week Ten**

Yogi concluded our orientation with a positive review to Josey, Dakota, and Amélie: "I see no safety concerns. He is going to do well and be an asset to the unit."

Josey said they would extend my orientation by two weeks "to get more comfortable."

Amélie tried to normalize it: "Don't let it worry you."

I asked directly if there was anything I should be working on. Josey said no—nothing specific.

Dakota said she had no concerns. Amélie agreed: I was doing fine—keep learning and asking questions. I left reassured.

Yogi's final notes: *addressed patient/family concerns; managed care effectively; communicated well with the team; good documentation; efficiently managed four to five patients.*

**Week Eleven**

I started night shift with Billie for two nights. She was kind, helpful, and practical—charting tips, blood draws, the small efficiencies that keep you afloat. Near the end of our second shift, she asked quietly, "You're with Robby next, right?"

"Yeah, starting tomorrow night. Anything I should know?"

Billie warned me, "Oh, Miles. Robby's... well, he's a piece of work. He likes to follow around all the young and pretty girls here on the unit. He's smart, sure. Knows his stuff. But he's got a reputation."

"What kind of reputation?"

She leaned in, lowering her voice. "He's... intense. Likes to test people. Sometimes he's more interested in showing off than teaching. And if you're not one of his favorites, he can be—let's just say—hard to please."

"Great. Any advice?"

"Don't take it personally. Seriously. He's tough on everyone, especially new grads. Just do your best, ask questions, and don't let him get under your skin. And if you need backup, you come find me, okay?"

"Thanks, Billie. I appreciate it."

She patted my shoulder. "You'll be fine. Just remember, you're not alone here."

***

I arrived at the nurses' station for my first shift with Robby. He was already there, leaning against the counter, flipping through a comic book. He wore a fitted muscle shirt that showed off a pink high-heeled shoe tattoo on his hip—a detail I had heard about but never seen up close. Robby looked up, his expression unreadable, then flashed a quick, practiced smile.

"Hey, you must be Miles," Robby said, casual—but edged. "You're with me tonight. I'll show you the ropes."

I nodded, trying to match Robby's energy. "Thanks. I'm ready to learn."

"Sorry you had to work with Billie. She's a crazy bitch."

I said nothing.

Robby closed his comic and tossed it onto the counter. "We've got four patients tonight. I'll be around, but you're running the show. If you need help, ask—but I expect you to figure things out."

"Okay."

The first two nights with Robby were uneventful—except Robby wasn't around much. "My work wife is here," he said, and disappeared with Laura while I handled the work.

When he realized my orientation had been extended, he grinned, shaking his head. "This is exactly why I love orientees—so you all can do all my work for me."

**Week Twelve**

I was reviewing the patient charts before passing medications, jotting down notes, while Robby watched silently. The silence was broken when he quizzed me in bursts—rapid-fire, situational, sometimes while he was half-texting.

"GI bleed. Plan?"

I started talking through it.

"No," he cut in. "Large bore IV, type and screen, prep for blood transfusion. You've gotta know this stuff cold."

Later, when I asked about a medication, he frowned. "You should know that by now. Look it up.

Near sunrise, he finally gave me a silver of praise: "Not bad. You'll get there. Just keep up."

***

As the nights went on, his tone sharpened. When he questioned me, he stood too close—close enough that I didn't need to lean to feel crowded. When my answers weren't what he wanted, he accused me of "lying," and that version of me started traveling upward to Josey.

While orientating with Robby, he informed me that he graduated with Josey from nursing school. He spent much time talking to Josey in her office, as our shifts would end prior to our weekly progress meetings; I also began to see them texting on his phone screen, when he was near me. He spoke much of his experiences at Dangerous Hospital, a trauma center in town, and talked about how orientating students and preceptees allowed him to read comic books and other novels. Recently, he had begun reading *The Dark Tower Series* by Steven King.

Robby's written feedback: *improve order tracking and attention to detail; strengthen report; don't give wrong information. "Becoming your own man." Noted improvement in report flow and watching orders.*

**Week Thirteen**

At the start of the week's first shift, Robby approached me with a wide, unsettling grin. "You'll want to read your emails before you start," he said, almost gleeful. "I'll take care of the patients while you read them. Take your time. Then come get me."

I logged into a computer-on-wheels and opened messages from Josey and Dakota. Each line landed like a blow. I started with Dakota's email.

*Miles,*

*I'm summarizing this morning's discussion with your preceptor, Robby. Key issues: understanding medication rationale, charting, and integrating information to understand each patient. These will be your focus for your upcoming nights of orientation with Robby.*

*The medication concern is knowing your medications and their implications—and being clear when you don't know something. This was one of the things Robby noticed in your practice and must be remediated prior to coming off orientation. Administering medications is serious and knowing each medication prior to administration is crucial in safe patient care.*

*Charting concern: copying and pasting. Robby reported you copied another nurse's note. Copying and pasting will not be tolerated. You must be able to chart independently and know what is important to incorporate into your charting. Copying and pasting from another RN's note is a huge liability for you and puts your patients at risk. The ability to chart effectively to outline what happened during your shift is so important.*

*Lastly, the concern about connecting everything together about each of your patients is critical in providing safe patient care. The ability to know the medications, administer medications, chart effectively and be able to tie everything together is a piece that is imperative in having before coming off orientation.*

*We'll meet again next week. These are serious concerns; if they aren't resolved, you will not come off orientation.*

I read Josey's email next.

*Miles,*

*Ongoing concerns persist: medication rationale, critical thinking, and copying/pasting notes. Because of these issues, we will extend your orientation by two additional weeks.*

*Support plan: reset to two patients on week one, then three, four, and five. We'll meet weekly with your preceptor and the union to evaluate your progress.*

*If you do not pass orientation, you may be referred to a Nursing Evaluation Committee that could result in disciplinary action up to separation from employment.*

# 8

At the start of the week, Josie announced a new set of paperwork requirements that would fundamentally change the rhythm of every shift. From now on, I was expected to complete detailed care plans for every patient, written with the same exhaustive thoroughness demanded of nursing students—mapping out diagnoses, interventions, and expected outcomes in painstaking detail. Alongside these, I had to fill out medication sheets for every single drug administered to every patient, even if the same medication was given for identical reasons across different cases. Each medication sheet required me to document the drug's normal dosage range, its clinical indications, and all potential adverse reactions.

No exceptions, no shortcuts. All of this paperwork was due at the end of every shift, adding hours of clerical work to days already stretched thin by the demands of patient care[1].

The changes Josey implemented made every shift harder. To keep patient care from taking a backseat, I rarely finished the required paperwork during the shift itself. Robby reviewed my care plans, threw them back at me, and told me to use medical diagnoses instead of nursing diagnoses—something nurses don't do. He said they were too "textbook."

To complete the care plans and medicine sheets completely, I spent three to four unpaid hours each week doing so at home—time taken away from sleep and family. I could complete the care plan portions of the sheets, but not all the medication parts due to time. This was necessary for it to be turned in by each weekly progress review.

Before administering any medication, I explained to Robby what it was and why I was giving it—every time. Though the added paperwork was excessive, it showed in writing that I knew what I was doing. None of that paperwork appeared in in the NEC evidence packet.

I never copied another nurse's note. With Robby's help, I created a blank template—history of present illness, assessment, and a systems-based plan—which I pasted into an empty note and filled out each shift.

A blank template is not the same as copying a nurse's note. I told them and proved to them that I was not copying and pasting anyone's note, and they didn't back down from their narrative. The paperwork and emails created a paper trail that made improvement impossible to document.

***

The clock blinked 2:17 a.m. after I read the emails extending my orientation again. The unit was quiet except for an occasional, ringing call light. I sat alone in the hallway next to my computer-on-wheels workstation, reviewing medication sheets, my clipboard open and pen poised.

Robby strode over, arms folded, a smirk playing at the edge of his mouth. He leaned in, too close, eyes scanning my notes.

"Quiz time," Robby said. "What's the gauge for the heparin needles on this unit?"

I glanced at my clipboard, nerves prickling. "Twenty-seven gauge. Gray cap."

Robby snorted. "You sure about that? You hesitated. You should know this by now. What's the angle for subcutaneous injection?"

"Ninety degrees," I replied, steadying my voice.

Robby shook his head. "You said fifteen degrees last week. Which is it? You can't keep guessing, man. This is basic stuff."

I felt my cheeks flush. "I corrected myself last time; I said the number of the computer-on-wheels I grabbed, because it was fresh on my mind. It's ninety degrees. I double-checked."

Robby rolled his eyes, flipping through my paperwork. "And what's the difference between Norco and Vicodin?"

I paused, searching my memory. "Both have hydrocodone and acetaminophen, but Norco has a higher acetaminophen content."

Robby tapped the desk, unimpressed. "Took you long enough. You're supposed to know this instantly. What if a patient asks you on the spot? You can't just look everything up."

I gripped my pen tighter. "I'd rather look it up than give the wrong answer."

Robby leaned in, voice dropping. "That's not good enough. You're on extended orientation. You should be teaching the new grads, not acting like one." He straightened, glancing at the clock. "I'll be watching your next med pass. Don't mess it up."

As Robby walked away, I felt my hands tremble. I stared at the clipboard, the words blurring. The lights above seemed harsher, the silence heavier. I took a slow breath, steadying myself, and returned to my charting-determined not to let Robby see me falter.

"I knew those emails would get to you," he called down the hall. "Knew they'd mess with your head." I hesitated, not sure if he expected a response or was just trying to rattle me further.

He stopped at the doorway of a patient's room down the hall, leaning against the frame with a sigh. "Honestly, I don't think I want to precept you anymore," Robby said. "It's not easy for either of us, and maybe someone else would be a better fit. I just needed to say that out loud."

The words hung in the air, heavier than before. I could feel my heart pounding as I tried to process what he'd just said, unsure of how to respond or what this meant for the rest of my orientation.

***

I was restless after noticing Robby's shift in attitude and how openly he'd said he didn't want to precept me. During our break, I decided to address it directly. I approached him during break. "Robby, can I talk to you for a minute?" I started, trying to sound calm.

He glanced up from his coffee, eyebrows raised. "Sure, what's up?"

I hesitated, searching for the right words. "I just want to know, do you have a personal issue with me? Because if you do, I'd appreciate some honesty. You don't have to keep precepting me if you don't want to. I want this to work, but I need to know where we stand."

Robby leaned back, considering this. "It's not personal, he said. "I'm pushing you to succeed."

I nodded, relieved. "Thanks for saying that. I want to get better and be someone this unit can count on. If I ever come off defensive, I'm just trying to learn."

Robby cracked a grin. "Keep at it. Ask questions, show up ready. That's all I want from you. You're going to be fine."

The tension eased, and I felt a little lighter heading back into the shift, determined to prove him right.

Robby's feedback: *know your meds and indications; attend call lights; work on confidence; don't make up answers; continue learning from everyone.*

***

I spent a lot of time talking to Sub, the union president. I informed him of how my orientation had gone with Sassy, my experiences with Yogi and Billie, and how things were going badly with Robby. I told him in his office, which was on the very top floor of the hospital and had a beautiful view of the mountains, of my concerns with how I was being presented and the false statements they were making about me and my performance.

Sub was chronically relaxed and cool. He scratched his soul patch atop his chin, which was his only facial hair. A gold Rolex watch was resting on his wrist of the hand he used to scratch himself.

He told me, "Well, I've talked to Josey, and she says she only has your best interests at heart and wants you to succeed. Let's just take this one week at a time. Do your thang, man. You're gonna be okay. I think this preceptor of yours is an ass-hole, but I don't think it's gonna cause us any trouble."

***

**Week Fourteen**

During a shift, I asked Robby to witness a narcotic waste. "My patient needs 0.5 mg in 0.5 mL IV push, so I'll waste half."

He stared at me. "How much are we *really* giving?"

"0.5 mg in 0.5 mL," I said—again.

We checked the order together. I was right. He didn't acknowledge it. "Next time, write it down," he said, then reported the interaction as if I hadn't known the dose.

***

The next night, at the nurses' station, Robby dropped a stack of comics over my notes.

"Difference between oxycodone and Percocet?"

"Percocet is oxycodone with acetaminophen," I said.

"You hesitated. You're going to hurt someone."

"No. I'm careful. I'd rather look something up than pretend."

He scoffed. "Safe nurses don't need to look things up after fourteen weeks."

I held eye contact. "Safe nurses don't disappear while their orientee carries five patients. If you have feedback, give it professionally. Otherwise, knock it off."

***

At the progress meeting, Robby had called in sick and was absent. When I sat down with Josey and Dakota, I said "Robby's treatment of me has crossed a line. I feel like I'm being bullied. I—"

Josey cut me off. "We're not here to discuss that. Let's stay focused."

She refused to change my preceptor.

Later, Josey called me on my day off to schedule an investigative interview.

***

I worked the rest of the week with Robby, same routine. After the next progress meeting, Robby was dismissed, and Josey began the investigative interview with Dakota assisting. Sub arrived just in time and sat beside me. Dakota and Josey were gathering papers and comparing them to one another quietly to themselves.

Sub glanced at me. "You okay? Do you know what this is about?"

"No," I said. "She didn't give me any details."

We sat in a small, windowless office. Josey cleared her throat. "This is a formal investigative interview regarding your orientation."

I nodded, trying to keep my hands from shaking.

Dakota leaned forward, her glasses catching the light. "How long have you worked for the HCO?"

"Five years."

"And at the hospital?" Josey asked.

"Five years."

Josey made a note, then looked up. "Describe your understanding of nursing orientation."

"You build from a small assignment to full load under a preceptor until you're signed off."

Dakota scribbled something on her pad. "And the role of an orienting nurse?"

"Learn under supervision."

Josey nodded. "And the role of a preceptor?"

"Teacher, mentor, and verify competency and safety."

Dakota's tone was neutral, almost clinical. "Why do we do progress meetings?"

"To track progress and address concerns."

Josey tapped her pen. "Your understanding of the extension?"

"More time to demonstrate safe practice."

Dakota's eyes narrowed. "What issues did management say you needed to resolve?"

"Medication knowledge, understanding the whole patient."

Josey flipped to another page. "What paperwork did you submit?"

"Medication sheets and care plans."

Dakota looked up. "Did you discuss the orientation email with Robby?"

"Not in depth."

Josey's tone sharpened. "Did you ask him to withhold concerns from management?"

"No."

"Did you ask him not to report that request?" Dakota pressed.

"No."

"What *did* you talk about?" Josey asked.

"I asked if he had a personal issue with me. He'd said he didn't want to precept me."

Josey's expression was unreadable. "Did you ask any other nurses to take over as your preceptor?"

"No."

Dakota set her pen down. "Anything you'd like to add?"

"I just want to do my job and learn."

Josey closed the folder. "Thank you. We'll review your responses and tell you the next steps."

9

In Sub's office, I said, "What the fuck are they doing? This isn't me. They're lying outright. I never said that to Robby."

Sub sighed. "I don't know. This is some mean-hearted shit."

"Can I transfer to another unit? I can't work there anymore."

"Calm down. Let's just see where this goes. Do your thang. Fill out the sheets. Don't lose your temper. Don't talk back. Cooperate—and sign what they tell you to sign."

"I can't keep signing things I don't agree with. It's bullshit."

Sub lowered his voice. "If you don't, they'll say you're uncooperative—a crazy war vet who can't cut it. That sticker on your badge? It doesn't help you out. Just cooperate."

I felt defeated.

***

Robby's creative feedback for Week 14: *Documented that a patient was admitted for laboratory monitoring. Stated that Tylenol was an NSAID. Continues to make up information; does not understand the whole patient.*

Josey's Week 14 email:

*Hi, Miles*

*I wanted to touch base regarding your performance during Week 14. I've noticed that your charting and patient-situation descriptions have shown improvement, which is a positive step forward. However, there was a slip-of-the-tongue noted regard-*

**Week Fifteen...**

...was the worst week. I wasn't eating. Sleep was rare. Nausea was constant. My anxiety peaked. Robby escalated—cornering me and saying, "People like you? We have ways of getting rid of nurses we don't want here."

His words stung, and he didn't stop there. "You're dangerous on this unit. You keep saying you know what you're doing, but you don't. Trust me, it would be safer for everyone if you just quit before you hurt someone."

I felt crushed—the pressure was unbearable, and Robby's constant undermining was pushing me deeper into self-doubt and fear for my future.

*****

That night, one patient had a draining hematoma and a distended abdomen from a bowel obstruction.

A small bowel obstruction, depending on the severity thereof, is often treated by gastric decompression with a nasogastric tube (NGT). The NGT is connected to a suction canister on the wall and set at an intermittent negative pressure to decompress the stomach and allow relief. Not doing so could compress the diaphragm upwards and potentially, compromise the patient's ability to breathe, which could lead to respiratory failure.

As we entered the room, I spotted blood seeping from the patient's hematoma. I glanced at the NGT suction and saw it was barely connected; I reattached it and restarted decompression.

"I'll call the on-call doc."

Robby delayed the call: "Clean him up first."

We changed the gown, started fluids, and he covered the patient with fresh blankets.

Then, he set the trap: "Go in there, look straight at him, and tell me what's wrong."

I checked out the patient and said, "I don't see anything out of the ordinary."

Robby's snapped. "He bled through his gown again. Didn't you notice?"

I pulled back the covers—blood again.

"The covers were over it," I said.

"You are lying!" he shouted—loud enough to turn heads. I changed the gown, reinforced the dressing, and called the physician.

***

Later, in an MRSA room, I didn't tie the back of my gown because I was only stepping to the doorway. Robby scolded me.

At the sink, he leaned in: "If your hand hygiene was poor and you passed MRSA next door—imagine if they were a neutropenic precautions patient and died. If that patient was a fellow Veteran, you'd have killed one of your own. How would you live with that?"

"That's not even possible. There isn't a neutropenic patient next door."

"Yeah, but you never know."

Jimmy—my close friend from the Army—had died by suicide not long before. The wound was still raw, which is why Robby's "fellow Veteran" line landed like a blade.

Neutropenic precautions are used in cancer patients and those who have low levels of white blood cells in the body to fight off infection. They aren't placed near contagious infections. That's why his scenario didn't apply.

***

When I gave Voltaren to a patient for topical pain relief, I measured it with a cup—Billie had shown me how after the measuring stick went missing. Later, Robby cornered me: "You didn't measure it."

"I did," I said.

He smiled. That's not how I remember it. Everyone else saw what happened. Maybe your confused."

For a moment, I found myself doubting my own memory—even though I knew exactly what I'd done.

Monica sent me to work with kimchi soup. I found my lunch bag on the floor—glass shattered inside. I threw it away and didn't tell her.

I couldn't eat or take a break. After vomiting three times, I finally broke down in the med room—hyperventilating, crying—my PTSD triggered for the first time since the Army.

"PTSD and anxiety sound like excuses," Robby said.

I wanted to go home. "I need to leave early."

He shrugged. "You can—but Josey and Dakota won't like it. It'll look weird."

I stayed.

Prior to the progress meeting, Robby told me, "Look, nobody believes anything you say. Josey and Dakota wonder at each of these meetings what you're going to lie about or try to cover up next, so you need to be honest with them about how this week went."

"I'm not lying or covering anything up. I'm going to tell them exactly how it went."

***

At the progress meeting, I said, "I have service-connected PTSD from my Army service."

Josey looked at me, uncertain how to respond, until Sub quietly encouraged her, "Josey, maybe you could let him know about the resources available?"

Sub prompted Josey to mention resources. Josey offered the Employee Help Program and told me to take care of myself.

Then, Robby pulled it back to his usual refrain: "Let's talk about your medication knowledge."

***

In Sub's office that day, he looked at me. "You look sick."

"I feel like it."

"One more week," he said. "Just one."

***

Josey's Week 15 email:

*Hi Miles,*

*I wanted to provide an update regarding my observations and concerns from Week 15 of orientation. I have noticed that* anxiety is impacting focus during shifts. There have also been infection-control concerns raised, including a specific claim about a neutropenic patient being in the adjacent room.

Additionally, there have been repeated issues related to medication knowledge, including questions around opioids, famotidine, heparin administration technique, simethicone, and Voltaren. Due to these ongoing medication-related concerns, I must conclude that orientation cannot be completed at this time.

Please let me know if you have any questions or need further details.

Best regards,

Josey

# 10

**Week Sixteen**

Before working my final weekend, I sought counseling. I came back with a thin layer of hope. The first night with Robby was the best yet. He told me I'd stayed on top of things and that my charting was "spot on." He rated me excellent across the board.

***

The next nights returned to the pattern: rapid-fire questions designed to catch me off balance.

"Mechanism of action for Metoprolol?"

"Beta blocker," I said. "It blocks beta receptors."

"False information," he replied. When I reached for my folding clipboard to verify, he snapped it shut over my hands. "You shouldn't need that."

***

On the final night, he set the hook: "Why does a prolonged QT matter in a Crohn's flare with vomiting and diarrhea?"

"I'm not telemetry certified yet," I said. "I haven't learned QT in depth."

"I know," he said. "Look it up tonight."

Then, he settled into the back of the station with his book and added, "Tonight's about you. Don't ask for help unless it's absolutely necessary."

The night swept me away—checking on other patients, updating charts, and finishing the mountain of extra paperwork that somehow always spilled over. By the end of my shift, I hadn't looked it up.

I received a patient with low BP in report, with notes indicating the team was aware and to notify only if it failed to improve before morning Carvedilol.

At 1:00 a.m., my Crohn's patient began retching and begged for relief. The only antiemetic ordered was IV Zofran, so I gave it, and her nausea eased. The order for Zofran had read for "severe nausea/vomiting not relieved by other antiemetic."

At 3:15, Robby asked, "Did you look up the QT question?"

"No," I said.

His voice sharpened. "Most antiemetics are contraindicated for patients with prolonged QT. You gave her Zofran?"

I called the cross-cover MD to update him. He wasn't concerned and said the "severe nausea/vomiting not relieved" clause was an intern mistake; he removed it.

Robby pressed me to tell Charity, the charge nurse, immediately. I told her I'd given Zofran to the patient with the QT warning.

Robby added loudly, "He was trying to cover it up. That's dishonest."

Later, he told me, "Charity says she can't trust you anymore."

When I spoke to Charity myself, she waved it off. "It's alright, Miles. Don't worry about it."

The patient's QT was about 420 milliseconds—hardly the dramatic "prolonged QT" Robby framed it as. No harm occurred.

***

After handoff, I slipped into an empty room with the lights off and cried.

Robby found me there. "You're good at this job," he said. "It's a shame I have to say otherwise, but you are damn good at this job."

"Then why did you do this to me?"

He stepped close, tucked finger to thumb, and thumped the "Military Veteran" sticker on my badge.

"Veterans only belong in the beds," he said, "not the bedside." He walked away to Josey's office to wait for me and Sub.

When I dried my tears and walked outside the room, Sub met me in the hall, smiling. "Congratulations—last week's done. Tell me good news!"

I shook my head.

"Shit," he said.

***

In the final progress meeting, Josey said, "Go ahead, Robby."

Robby stared at his shoes. "We had somewhere to get over these four weeks, and...we just never got there."

Sub finally snapped. "Robby, you're being a real nut-job. Did you know every med you ever gave before you gave it, without looking anything up?"

Josey ignored him. When Sub finished, she said, "Thanks, Robby. You can go."

Then, she scheduled a meeting "to discuss steps going forward."

***

Josey's final email framed the weekend as a medication failure:

*Miles,*

*After reviewing the events of this past weekend, I must document that there was a significant medication-related issue. Specifically, it appears that you did not demonstrate understanding of the QT interval significance and proceeded to administer Zofran despite a clear, bold red warning in the MAR. Additionally, it was noted that you withheld important information from the charge nurse, which I must characterize as deceptive.*

*Given these concerns, we cannot permit you to work independently at this time. We will be discussing next steps with the union and Human Resources to determine the appropriate course of action.*

*Sincerely,*

*Josey*

***

**The Final Meeting**

Later that day, I was copied on an email from Josey to Kelly:

*Kelly,*

*We have reviewed the documentation from Miles's orientation period, and from this review, we would like to recommend a Nursing Evaluation Committee. The case file is prepared for your review.*

***

Sub and I met with Dakota and Josey in Dakota's office. HR—Mr. Dipsitt—joined by speaker phone. Josey said, "We've reviewed your orientation and file. We're recommending a Nursing Evaluation Committee to determine the next steps."

Sub said, "An NEC is not necessary! The union recommends a transfer. That's what fixes this."

Mr. Dipsitt said, "I reviewed the file. It shows ongoing problems that were never corrected. I support the NEC. They went above and beyond to try to help him."

Sub snapped. "Above and beyond, my ass. You are judging him like a five-year nurse. A transfer fixes this."

"The NEC will decide," Mr. Dipsitt said. "That's the process."

Sub stood. "Then there's nothing else to talk about. Let's go, Miles." He led me out.

In Sub's office, he handed me an NEC packet. Every example inside ended the same way: separation.

Sub picked up the phone and called Josey. "Josey, is it okay for Miles to take paid time off for the rest of the week?"

I heard Josey reply on the speaker, "Yes, that's fine. Miles can return next Monday."

"You'll report Monday," Sub said. "Administrative duties in a cubicle until the NEC decides."

# 11

Two weeks later, Serenity—the NEC president—reached out with a suggestion: report to the replacement hospital's administration building instead of my usual area, to avoid humiliating run-ins while the committee deliberated. I agreed, relieved by the small mercy.

Serenity told me the NEC was "non-adversarial": if I was let go, there would be no report to the licensing board, and confidentiality would be protected. The committee would review both evidence packets, hear my statement, ask questions, then vote on transfer or separation.

***

Sub and I received the evidence packet—emails and progress reports from Josey and Dakota. The cover was neon pink, stamped in black: *EVIDENCE FILE: DO NOT CHANGE!*

Inside was an email from Robby to Josey, sent before the investigative interview. Robby wrote:

*Miles asked me in the break room not to report negative incidents from his orientation to Dakota and Josey. I told him I'd continue to inform them if things don't improve, but I wouldn't share every minor detail.*

*I told Miles that his extended orientation is to help him improve. I explained that if I ignore issues like underperformance or unsafe practices, it risks patient safety, undermines management's trust, and burdens other nurses.*

*After this, he appeared to grasp the situation. He requested that I not inform you (Josey and Dakota) about our discussion. At the time, I agreed not to mention it. However, as I reflected on it, I realized the importance of bringing this matter to management's attention and decided it needed to be discussed.*

There was another email from Robby to Josey.

*When Miles administered heparin, he couldn't specify the correct gauge, route, or angle; he answered "15 degrees" but did not mention subcutaneous administration.*

*I've seen sources recommend 45–90 degrees. I always ask students about current guidelines, so it was concerning that he didn't know the correct technique for administering heparin, our most common medication.*

*I often have students or orientees enter a friendly patient's room to assess for anything needing attention, as long as it isn't urgent. With Miles's patient, who had a recently drained hematoma and other issues including a potential ICU transfer, I asked Miles about his next steps after we left the room.*

*He started cleaning the faulty suction unit we'd removed, but I pointed out our patient was covered in blood and asked if that should be our priority. He agreed, and we addressed the patient's condition first.*

*Later, we administered IV fluids and medication to the patient, after which he left the room. Outside, I suggested going back in and taking some time to observe if there was anything else we needed to address before leaving. He didn't notice anything. So, I pointed out that the patient had bled through his gown.*

*Miles returned to the room to address the issue and then exited. I was not concerned that Miles had overlooked blood on the patient's gown, as it is understood that oversights can occur. However, upon leaving the room, he explained that he had not noticed the bleeding because it was "covered up."*

*I responded, "If that is the case, how was I able to notice it?" I was concerned that an excuse was given rather than acknowledging the oversight regarding the patient gown, which had a significant amount of blood on it. Observing this situation, I question Miles's clinical proficiency and his willingness to seek out information when necessary.*

*I also doubt his integrity and feel compelled to supervise him more carefully since he refuses to acknowledge his mistakes. Does this behavior truly reflect who he is as a nurse? How might he conduct himself if I were not present?*

The email framed my actions as evasive rather than corrective.

***

I submitted my evidence to the NEC prior to the deadline they gave me, which included my performance reviews from past jobs and nursing school clinical rotations, the character statement letters, my written response to the NEC, and my written timeline of events.

Another email was added after Josey's evidence deadline.

*While precepting Miles, we worked with several PCAs. On one occasion, a patient's PCA syringe ran empty. Since I was unavailable, he asked Carli, RN, to help replace it.*

*Soon after, the patient called to report medication leaking from the machine. I found the PCA syringe tip broken and the tubing wrapped around it. After fixing it, I asked Carli if she had changed the syringe or documented on the flow sheet; she said Miles changed the syringe while she handled the paper-work.*

*I saw Carli's handwriting on the PCA flow sheet, not Miles's. I informed Miles about the PCA leak and broken tip; he said Carli changed the PCA while he filled out the flowsheet. Let me know if you need more details. I'm unsure of the exact date.*

Thanks,

Sassy

No narcotics discrepancy report existed. Narcotics leaking all over the place would not have been mopped up and forgotten about. All narcotics were accounted for judiciously.

***

Until the very end, Sub insisted the right thing to do was not to talk back, fight back, or appear uncooperative. Sub later told me he regretted telling me to sign the reports.

I was also defeated. I complied when I shouldn't have. I trusted advice that failed me. I never went in to talk to Josey one on one, and I wish I had.

I think back and wonder if it would have helped had I asked her for a private word and said something like this:

"I understand I wasn't who you wanted. This isn't a good fit. If transfer isn't possible, I'll resign. Does that work?"

I never said this to her, but it feels good to put it in writing.

***

The last thing Josey gave me was a progress report to sign. She wrote:

*Miles completed his RN program at Awesome University and started as a new graduate nurse on That Unit. The management and education teams designed a twelve-week progres-*

sive orientation plan for him, meeting every two weeks with Miles and his primary preceptor to review his progress. Initially, Miles handled 2-3 patients well, but soon began showing concerning practice behaviors, such as not understanding or researching medications and lacking critical thinking skills. Despite ongoing education and remediation from his preceptor and educator, these mistakes persisted week after week. His integrity was also questioned when he blamed an experienced nurse for a mistake he made involving a PCA. His preceptor expressed concerns to both Miles and management.

Miles later told management and education that he had a personality conflict with his preceptor, so management assigned him a new preceptor. However, even with this change and additional support from the unit educator, issues continued with Miles's critical thinking and medication administration. He also struggled to understand patient diagnoses and articulate proper care plans. After ten weeks, as Miles prepared to begin night shifts, management extended his orientation by two weeks because many concerns remained. Working nights with another experienced preceptor, it quickly became evident that further extension was needed. Following consultation with the union, management agreed to extend Miles's orientation for another two weeks, totaling four months—one month longer than usual for new nurses.

During the four-week extension, progress meetings increased to weekly intervals, encouraging collaboration among Miles, his preceptor, the union, and management. Miles's clinical nurse educator introduced a medication review form and a plan of care worksheet for him to complete each shift. Nevertheless, Miles's understanding of medication administration and crit-

*ical thinking did not improve, and his new preceptor continued raising concerns about his integrity. Although Miles's documentation improved—he stopped copying and pasting notes—he kept making recurring mistakes in medication administration and critical thinking during weeks 15 and 16, such as not understanding differences between narcotics, struggling to administer subcutaneous heparin despite repeated instruction, and giving Zofran to a patient with a prolonged QT interval against both preceptor prompts and physician warnings.*

*Due to serious concerns about patient safety and Miles's continued unsatisfactory performance over his 16-week orientation, he was unable to demonstrate safe, competent care, despite extended support from management, his preceptors, and the unit educator.*

I had had enough at this point. I wrote: "I acknowledge receipt of this form. I DO NOT agree with this assessment." I then handed it back to Josey, who looked genuinely shocked. I turned my back from her and walked away. I never saw her again.

***

**The Day of the NEC**

One month after my orientation ended, I waited outside a conference room. Five NEC members would hear my statement, ask questions, then vote. A majority vote would decide my future.

Sarah, the union vice president, sat beside me. She had reviewed my evidence and helped me prepare.

The panel included Serenity (president), Joelle from Nursing Informatics, Tina—a charge nurse from That Unit,

Andie—an assistant nurse manager from Step-Down, and one final member we hadn't been told about.

The door opened. Sassy and Tom stepped in.

"What's Miles doing here?" Tom asked.

Serenity stood. "Wrong room. Charge nurse meeting is upstairs." They apologized and left.

Then Les walked in. He'd written my recommendation letter for nursing school. We'd also been close and worked together in the ICU when I was an RT. Seeing him there hurt.

I sat at the end of a long conference table, my hands folded tightly in my lap. The room was quiet except for the shuffle of papers. The five members of the NEC looked at me with a mix of professionalism and empathy. Sarah looked over and offered a reassuring nod.

Serenity said, "Miles, you can begin your verbal response whenever you're ready."

I took a steadying breath and began, my voice trembling slightly. "I want to thank you for giving me the chance to speak. I served in the Army, then worked here as an RT before becoming a nurse through the scholarship program. Everywhere else, I was supported and treated fairly. On That Unit, I wasn't. I struggled—not because I was unsafe, but because the environment became hostile. I'm asking to continue my career here. I know I can succeed."

My eyes welled up as I spoke. "I just want you to know that, before all this, my career at this hospital was on track—I was proud to work alongside nurses like you. I feel incredibly privileged to be here. Please, I'm asking you—let me continue my career at this hospital. I know I can succeed if given the chance."

When I finished, several members were visibly emotional. Tina looked down. Sarah rested a hand on my arm.

Serenity said, "We've reviewed both evidence packets. We don't see that you did anything wrong. You didn't hurt anyone. So, before we ask you some questions, I want you to take a breath and relax."

I took a few breaths and steadied myself as the silence marinated the air. I looked back at Serenity. I gave her a nod that I was ready.

Serenity began. "Miles, thank you for coming in today. We've reviewed your written statement and the evidence from both sides. Thank you as well for your verbal response just now. Next, we'd like to ask you a few questions before we make our decision."

I nodded, my throat dry. "Of course."

Joelle leaned forward. "Describe your experience on That Unit"

"It started well. Sassy was supportive at first, but things changed. Some of her feedback didn't match what actually happened. Yogi was a great mentor. With Robby, it became aggressive. I felt bullied."

Tina asked gently, "Did you ever feel unsupported by management?"

"Yes."

Andie spoke next. "How did this affect your performance and your health?"

"It affected my health. My anxiety escalated, and my PTSD was triggered."

Les looked me in the eye. "Did you ever compromise patient safety?"

"No. I double-checked, asked for help and looked things up."

Serenity offered a kind smile. "Why do you think things went the way they did?"

"A narrative formed early. Once it did, everything was filtered through it. I trusted the process. I wish I hadn't signed things I did, and I wish I'd spoken up for myself sooner."

Sarah squeezed my arm, and I felt a surge of gratitude.

Serenity closed her folder. "Thank you, Miles. We'll confer and let you know our decision."

I nodded, tears stinging my eyes. As I left the room, I felt a strange mix of relief and dread—knowing I'd finally told my story, but uncertain what would come next.

I would learn the NEC's decision from Kelly a month later in the HR building.

By the time I found myself sitting outside that HR office in October, I had already lived through all of it.

# PART IV: THE TURNING PAGE

# 12

L ater—the week after we had returned from Texas, I was seeing double after 3 dark beers. I'd given Earl all the evidence and re-read it myself, trying to make sense of it. Having recently worked on a high-acuity unit, I could see that my orientation on That Unit had been designed for my exit. There was no other explanation. He-said-she-said doesn't survive on functional units—no one has time for it.

A nurse named Dave rapidly bolused potassium chloride instead of fluids and killed a patient. Josey had hired him and liked him. Afterward, there were no investigations—just silence.

My phone rang just at the peak of the buzz. Earl's voice cut through. "Well, that mess was every bit as depressing as I thought it'd be," he admitted. "Started out reading it over Texas tea but had to switch to Long Island Iced just to get through it." No matter how rough things got, he could still make me laugh—something I badly needed.

I leveled with Earl. "I've twisted myself in knots trying to figure out what happened and why. I just want to forget it and get back to the ICU. I trained in the ICU during school at LTH. Hell, I'm at LTH now, because they left me no choice. They booted me on Veteran's Day, of all days. Now the big HCO want to pin it on me?"

Earl shot back, "Big HCO doesn't want any of that. I'm big HCO's guy, you know. They just want you back on the job. They're not happy about what went down, but their focus is getting you working for them again."

"What about the folks who put me in this spot? I've got roots here, a home, a community. Now I'm packing up to leave while my wife is stuck here finishing nursing school. We're stuck dealing with what THEY did!"

Earl knew how to let me get it all out, then nudge me forward when others would just shut down. "You're right, son. But let big HCO handle the ones who did you wrong. Let me help you move forward. Let's get you prepped for your interviews. You've got a shot at the hospital in Coffee, Washington for ICU and at Big City, Texas in Spinal Cord Injury. Get back out there, and I know good things are coming your way."

"And Mountainton?" I asked.

He laughed. "Forget about them. Sure, you can apply and interview again, but they're never gonna hire you. And even if they did, they'd find some excuse—say you can't even tie your own shoes—and you'd just end up back in the same mess or worse. Trust me, Texas'll suit you."

Over the next month, I followed Earl's lead and interviewed at HCO hospitals in Coffee, Big City, and Mountainton.

***

The Coffee ICU was exactly the kind of place I'd pictured myself thriving—a unit known for teamwork, high standards, and a genuine sense of camaraderie. I had worked with nurses who had worked there and loved it. For my interview, via Facetime, I met Dr. Chan, the ICU medical director, and Sam, the nurse manager.

"Miles, we've heard great things about you," Dr. Chan began, "but we'd love to hear what drew you to our ICU here in Coffee."

I sat a little straighter. "Honestly, the way you care for each other here stands out. Every nurse I've spoken to says this is a place where you're challenged, but you never feel alone. That's what I want—a space to grow, contribute, and to learn from the best."

Sam nodded, jotting a note. "We believe in mentoring here. What's one challenge you've faced that shaped who you are as a nurse?"

I took a breath. "In my first unit, I faced intense scrutiny. It taught me resilience and the importance of advocating for my patients and myself. Even when things got tough, I never compromised on safety or integrity. I've learned how vital it is to ask questions and lean on my team. That's why I'm drawn here—to be part of a unit where those values matter."

Dr. Chan smiled. "That's what we're looking for. Collaboration isn't just a word—it's our daily reality. Do you have any questions for us?"

I leaned forward at my iPad, eager. "I'd love to hear more about your mentoring program and what successful transition looks like for nurses new to the ICU here."

Sam and Dr. Chan exchanged a glance. "We match every new nurse with an experienced mentor. The goal is to build confidence and skill, but also to create trust. Many of our strongest team members started just where you are now."

As the interview wrapped up, I felt a rush of excitement. The Coffee ICU felt like home—the kind of place that would support my growth and passion for critical care. I caught my-self smiling.

***

The Big City people were nice, but I had no desire to be in Spinal Cord Injury (SCI) for the simple matter that I felt it was in the way of my overall goals.

Lydia, the Big City Medical Center's SCI nurse manager, greeted me via FaceTime with a warm smile. Her energy was welcoming, almost infectious, and she chatted me up about the latest renovations and the team's camaraderie. Her posture was open and relaxed.

"So, tell me what draws you to Spinal Cord Injury nursing," Lydia asked, her tone genuinely interested, eyes sparkling with encouragement.

I returned her smile, careful to keep my nerves and reservations tucked away. "I've always admired the complexity and dedication that goes into caring for SCI patients. There's a lot to learn, and the teamwork here sounds incredible."

She nodded, leaning in, clearly eager to highlight her unit's strengths. "We're really proud of our collaborative environment. Nurses have a voice, and we work closely with our therapists and physicians. It's challenging but rewarding in ways that surprise you."

I listened intently, knowing this wasn't where I wanted to land.

***

I had applied to a new unit at the replacement hospital for Mountainton's hospital, located in Wylde Town Falls. When I arrived, I realized, much to my surprise, that the new unit was exactly the same one I'd left. As I walked into the interview room, I saw Dakota and Amélie waiting for me.

Dakota leaned forward, her voice cool and steady. "Welcome back," she said, exchanging glances with Amélie. "It's been a while."

Amélie added, "So, what brings you to Wylde Town Falls? Looking for a fresh start?"

I swallowed, feeling the tension rising. "I wanted to find a place where I could really contribute—and this seemed like the right fit."

Their expressions didn't soften. They stared at me with unsettling intensity, reminding me of the *Stepford Wives*—polite, but almost chilling. I met their gaze, refusing to look away. I hoped they could see I wasn't backing down, even if my words were few.

The new hospital itself was spotless and modern. "The place looks great," I commented, genuinely impressed.

Dakota gave a small, tight smile. "We're proud of it."

Inside, I wished I could work there, despite the coldness of the interview. But in the end, I was relieved that things didn't go that way.

***

A month later, Mountainton declined my application. That same day, Coffee called.

"If you reapply next quarter, you're in," Sam assured me over the phone. "But this time, we have to hire internally."

Later, Big City reached out with an offer, which I'd heard via voicemail. I took the news to Earl.

"Big City made an offer," I told him.

Earl didn't hesitate. "Take it," he said firmly.

I frowned. "But Coffee said they'd hire me next quarter. Can't I wait for them?"

Earl didn't hesitate. "You know the HCO's deadline. You've got until the end of their fiscal year to sign on. Big City can get you in by then. Coffee can't."

I let out a sigh, conflicted but knowing Earl was right.

Earl sensed my hesitation. "You can't let this get in your head. Those people who did this—they don't know what they're talking about. To be honest, they're some dumb motherfuckers, son. You did everything you could. You told the truth, you stood your ground, and you did what was right."

I just listened, still.

"Now, let all that go," Earl continued, his voice steady. "You did your part, and you made sure the right people heard what needed saying. It's time to focus ahead, not back. Texas is waiting."

Earl's words settled over me. I nodded, realizing he was right. There was no use in perseverating on what couldn't be changed. I took a breath, resolved to trust the path before me, and let go of my fear. I'd done everything I could—I had been honest, and now it was time to move forward.

Elvis Presley once said, "Truth is like the sun. You can shut it out for a time, but it ain't goin' away." The truth is this—those dumb motherfuckers were wrong about me.

# 13

Goodbyes were never easy, and this one felt like a gut punch. Marge, especially, was going to be hard to leave. Up until now, the road hadn't exactly been paved with gold. I was caught in a strange crosscurrent—on one hand, I was finally enjoying what Trauma Drama had given me; on the other, I felt sick knowing I'd accepted a job that would send me back into the HCO, this time in Texas.

It wasn't the straightest path toward my goals, but I had to believe it was happening for a reason. No job had ever come this easily to me. The application was simple. The interview felt effortless. That alone should have told me something.

The hard part came during onboarding. The HR rep in Texas—Del—was a Veteran. When he greeted me with, "Welcome back to the HCO, brother," I realized how long it had been since anyone had spoken to me like that. Everyone I interacted with was kind. Genuinely kind. Somewhere along the way, I realized that maybe I didn't need to be suspicious of that anymore.

Unlike other organizations, the HCO has added questions after one has accepted a job offer that one must answer while onboarding. To say they are overly secure is an understatement. Many of the questions were no-brainer yes or no questions such as "Have you ever been arrested/convicted/indicted?" Then came the one that made my chest tighten: "Have you been terminated or released from a job within the last five years?"

At LTH, I hadn't yet been let go, so I'd never had to answer *yes* before. I asked Earl what to do. "Tell the truth," he said. "Don't worry about the rest." I worried anyway.

The deadline of having to have secured a job with the HCO, lest I be monetarily penalized, was getting closer. Worry and dread set in. I could see how this would play out in the worst way: I answer yes, it raises an alarm, someone talks to someone else, the offer is rescinded, and I lose my ass financially paying them back for the scholarship.

Best case was maybe they let me go back to square one with Earl and search elsewhere for an HCO job. However, I worried it might be in a worse place than the option I had. There were certainly worse places the HCO had to offer. I remembered a friend of mine landing in Deliverance, Kentucky to pay back his scholarship time.

Winter had returned. Snow fell again, just like it had the day Kelly let me go in that dilapidated HR building. I thought about how beautiful the summer had been—and how little of it I'd truly enjoyed under the weight of what was coming. I wish I'd hiked more.

I told the truth on the questionnaire. Things were nearly done with the onboarding process. Del emailed me, asking for more detail about the separation. *Just for the file*, he said. My dad helped me write the response.

*To Whom It May Concern:*

*Thank you for the opportunity to interview for the position of Registered Nurse with the Big City Medical Center and for the tentative offer.*

*This letter is in response to the request that information be provided about the departure from my earlier employer, the*

Mountainton Medical Center after five years of employment there.

A brief time prior to my separation from the above, I was placed onto a nursing unit after I had graduated nursing school via the HCO Scholarship Program and become an RN. Members of the unit disclosed to me management's dissatisfaction with my being placed there due to their desire to hire someone else in the position. Per HCO Scholarship Program guidelines, my placement there was something neither I nor the unit's management could control.

I completed day shift orientation under the guidance of many preceptors (nurses who train one to their new unit). Dayshift orientation was ten weeks. I was then to complete two weeks of orientation to nightshift prior to practicing independently.

Nightshift orientation saw me working with a male nurse preceptor. He told me, "On this unit, we have ways of making people go away if we don't want them." He made false reports to the manager about performance deficiencies and accused me of asking him not to report them.

The manager extended my orientation with him as my preceptor for four added weeks. My attempts to tell my side were disregarded. From that time forward, tension in my relationship between my manager, the preceptor, and myself increased.

This preceptor was astonished that I did not quit despite him subjecting me to sustained workplace violence. He said that I was good at my job, but I had to be portrayed as otherwise. When I asked why, he told me, "Veterans only belong here as patients and not as nurses."

*My manager wrote a poor performance review of me created from a false narrative. She then sent me to a Nursing Evaluation Committee. They sided with her and voted for non-adversarial separation during my probationary period, effective Veterans Day.*

*I was told by an HR representative that I was being separated, because the unit had wanted to hire someone else in my position. This was again said to me by the very person who processed my paperwork. I was also told that I was re-hirable.*

*As you will note from my application and from my references, my professional record of accomplishment illustrates a sound employment history. The isolated incident at the Mountainton Medical Center was beyond my control. This event does not reflect the circumstances or opinion of any other prior or current employer, which you are welcome to verify.*

*I appreciate the opportunity to explain this event. Again, I'm grateful for the interview and prospect of working for the Big City Medical Center.*

*Sincerely,*

*Miles, BSN, RN, RRT*

***

Dad always knew how to say the hard things clearly—without venom, without apology. When Del replied, it was immediate, via phone. "Wow. I'm so sorry this happened to you. I can't change the past, but I can help change the path forward. I'm going to put this with your file and give it to our senior nurse officer here for final sign off. Don't worry, I will make sure she has a full picture of who you really are. The hard part is over. Right now, let's get you back into the HCO. I'll be in touch."

I didn't realize how much I needed to hear that until my vision blurred.

***

My remaining time on Trauma Drama was chaos, beauty, and exhaustion braided together. The kind of days that remind you why this work matters. Days went by, and like all things, I let it go with reckless abandon even though the inevitable was approaching fast.

I was having a busy shift from hell on Trauma Drama. I had a young woman as a patient, who was very violent and had a developmental delay. She was 26 and had the mind of an angry 5-year-old with a body builder's strength. She had had issues with stomach cancer and required an ileostomy placement—a bag outside her body to collect her stool.

In her room, we had a tele-sitter, which was a tall, HAL-9000-looking device. It was simply a tower on wheels with a camera on top of the tower. Someone was at the other end of the device watching, and they would speak to the patient to remind her not to get out of bed or to call a nurse. The patient's mother happened to be in the room with her, and one of my nurse's aides was in the room as well to help her with a lunch tray.

At the same time, I had a very colorful patient who had gotten into a fight with police SWAT while holding up a convenience store. He had a .38 special revolver pistol and walked outside to engage the SWAT team who were atop the hill with their rifles trained on him; he lost badly. When they inevitably opened fire, he turned to his right side and put up his left arm to protect himself. His left arm, hip, and leg took most of the fire and resulted in broken bones requiring surgery and then a full limb cast on the arm and leg. I had to use cotton-tipped swabs—long, tall Q-tips—to pack moist gauze into his deep stomach wounds, which had miraculously missed his organs.

He was on a Dilaudid PCA and additional IV push pain medications. I went to get him the additional medications after packing his wounds. While another nurse was wasting the unnecessary part of the extra Dilaudid IV push with me in the medication room, my patient had decided to carry out a more sinister event.

I walked out of the medication room with my meds in hand and walked down the hall towards his room. I saw the two police officers, who had been playing Angry Birds on their iPads while sitting guard outside of his room, drop their iPads and run into his room suddenly with their guns drawn. I froze in place, expecting to hear POP! POP! POP! POP! POP! POP! POP! POP! followed by the screams of the staff and visitors around.

Nickel was what we call a "terminal" Certified Nurse Assistant (CNA). She was 55 years old, tall, gruff, and had a smoker's voice. She grunted when exerting herself to move things or boost patients up in bed.

My wild, would-be shooter patient had the brilliant idea that he and Nickel were close enough to the same size after sizing her up. He knew the officers guarding him had such a boring detail, they didn't bother to cuff him to the bed. Given that he had a hard cast covering his left arm from bicep to fingers and a hard cast covering his left leg from thigh to toes, their assumption was reasonable. The officers got to be very proficient playing Angry Birds and Candy Crush on their iPads during this detail.

On this day, the patient rang his call light to ask for help going to sit on the toilet, and Nickel answered. He was completely naked, so Nickel, like any good caregiver, pulled the curtains to give him privacy, and the guards didn't notice at first that their view was obstructed. Nickel was going to have him lean on her with his good side, and they would hobble over to a bedside toilet. The patient decided to take his sinister initiative.

Using his casted arm, he hooked his arm around Nickel's neck with her chin and throat at his elbow's corner. With his good right arm, he pushed her head forward to attempt to choke her out. He didn't count on this powerful, big girl putting up such a fight. She grunted, struggled, and managed to make noise by kicking over his bedside tray table.

The police, per their words, heard her doing "that grunt she does," and they knew something was wrong. They then went running in with their guns drawn. I heard the commotion, thuds, and screaming from outside the room, and I stopped in place.

My jolly charge nurse, Jess, saw me standing there in the hallway with narcotics in hand, and a scared look on my face, so she approached to help. Jess was impeccably positive, and despite being the black cloud at work, she made everyone at work happy. She was radiant and about 8 months pregnant with her first kid. Even so, she was like a mom to all of us already.

"Hey there, Milesy," she said. "Watcha doin' there with that Dilaudid?"

"Well," I told her, "I was about to go give it to my prisoner patient, but the cops jumped up and ran in there with their guns out. I'm not sure what's going on."

"Well, fluff my feathers, Milesy." The next thing we knew, cops were appearing from the stairways along with security guards, and they were all rushing into the room.

Like a good charge nurse, Jess took the initiative. "I think we should go waste that Dilaudid in the med room, Milesy. I don't think he's gonna get that. Who knows if he even has an IV still." We went into the med room and did just that.

Luckily, the police had saved Nickel's life. She was in a cervical collar for a while and got to do secretary work until she got promoted to a new administrative position that was created for her. The police had gone into the room with their guns drawn and yelled at my patient to let her go.

Ever the bright thinker, he thought he could use Nickel as a human missile, launch her at the officers like a bowling ball, knock them down like bowling pins, and make his miraculous escape. He succeeded in knocking down one of the officers, who went tumbling with Nickel. The other officer speared him like a Georgia linebacker and out came the man's two IVs. This meant no immediate Dilaudid and no more PCA for him. The man spent the rest of that time cuffed to the bed by both wrists and both feet.

These series of events ran through lunch, and I scarfed a Kind Bar. We carried mobile phones, provided by the hospital, to better hasten communication between us and the care team. It was awesome, except when one's day got crazy busy. My phone rang while I was catching up on charting about the morning's mayhem. The tele-sitter from my developmentally delayed patient was on the line, and he said what no nurse ever wants to hear.

"Hey, this is Ned, the tele sitter for your patient. Sorry to bother you, but I was at the bathroom for just a minute, and since I came back, I don't see your patient anywhere."

WHAT?! "What do you mean?!," I asked. At that moment, I jumped up and ran to her room. I saw a scene not unlike the Texas Chainsaw Massacre.

Blood streaks aligned the floor and the walls along with stool. The smell of blood and feces was in the air. A discarded ostomy bag was smashed onto the wall and sliding down like a pancake.

The patient's mother was moaning on the floor and holding her shoulder, which was freshly slashed. My CNA for her room, Emmy, was on the floor as well, holding her freshly slashed hand and crying. Next to her was the patient's shattered ceramic plate, missing a large, jagged piece. The tele-sitter tower was on the floor, having been knocked down. I was about to assess the patient's mother and Emmy, when I heard the grunting roar of my patient from down the hall at the end followed by screams of the visitors and the other patients.

At the end of the hall, I saw the flash of my patient's quick movement, and her discarded patient gown seemed to float to the floor from the air above. I heard her footsteps running across the hall distant to me where the family conference room was at the hallway's end, facing the mountains. There were bloody handprints decorating the walls. The overworked security guards ran past me to confront my now nude and bloodied, crazed patient in the family conference room.

She was armed with the missing jagged piece of shattered ceramic plate. I heard the guards scream, "I'm gonna fucking taze you! Drop that fucking thing right now!" She did just that, and the chaos was over.

Jess held her mouth and retched as she called housekeeping to come and clean up the bloody mess that had the residual smell of stool in the air. I sat down at the computer next to her charge computer to chart and we just exhaled and silently laughed with one another, because we couldn't do anything else to respond to the situation.

My prisoner patient's call light rang, and I went to see what he needed. Cody was in the room putting in new IV's so that I could give medicines when needed. He greeted me, "Fucking crazy ass shit today right bro?! Fuck!"

I replied, "Yep," and I asked the patient, "How can I help you?"

"I don't feel good!" Was all he said before he did the cherry on top of my wild day.

Jess had followed me into the room, wanting to be on top of what was up with this guy considering today's events. Unfortunately for her, she walked in immediately after he told me he didn't feel good. He projectile vomited blood, and she immediately projectile vomited her breakfast and lunch afterwards into the hallway. God, I was gonna miss this unit.

***

It was nearing the end of the day when my phone rang, and I slipped into the bathroom to take the call. Del was calling from Big City Medical Center. My heart stopped for a moment.

"Miles," Del said, "you made it. You're back in the HCO."

I was in such a shock, I didn't notice that tears had filled my eyes, my nostrils, and run into my mouth until my vision was blurred and I tasted salt. I cried in that hospital bathroom like a child who'd finally been told they were safe. Del heard it from his end of the phone.

"Wow," was all I could say. "I can't believe it."

Del chuckled and said, "You did it, Miles. You beat those assholes. You're coming home to the HCO. We're lucky to have you and to get you back."

My breath was trembling, and I was sniffling still. "Thank you, Del," I started. "Thank you, I don't know how to… just thank you."

"My pleasure, Miles," he told me. "Remember, you've been through a lot to get where you are. If you focus and hold your head high, there's nothing you can't accomplish. You have the right environment to do that now, so do it."

"Does anyone know about Mountainton?" I asked him, and I heard myself crying through my own voice as if something else had taken over my body like a tidal wave of emotion.

"No, no," he said. "The senior nurse officer here is good. She's really good, and she was touched by your story. She's going to make sure your privacy is protected. That wasn't anyone else's place to tell anyway."

"Okay," I replied, and I began to slow down my breathing.

Del worked with me to push my start date out as far as reasonably possible. Monica would stay with her sister and her husband as she finished her final semester of nursing school at Awesome University. I would move to Big City, Texas with our two golden doodles in an apartment to start, and our house in Mountainton would be sold.

After we had moved to Mountainton, we allowed Monica's younger sister, Phoebe, to come and live with us so that she could pursue her college education and make a life over here. Through Phoebe I got to learn the joy and love of having a little sister, as I had lost that long ago with my own. I wouldn't hesitate to pull an extra shift here and there to make sure she never missed a birthday cake, or a Christmas present she'd wanted.

I didn't know it at the time, but this solidified the foundation of love and respect between my extended family and me. Phoebe met and married a man whom I am privileged to call my brother-in-law. I'm so eternally grateful to them for helping us out by letting Monica stay with them while she finished nursing school, and I had to move early.

# 14

Saying goodbye to Marge nearly broke me. The sky over Wylde Town Falls was still a bruised shade of gray when I walked into Trauma Drama early for a shift. The unit was the kind of quiet that only happens right before the day shift storms in. I dropped my bag in the locker room, then saw Marge at the far end of the hall, looking at her phone with her glasses low on her nose.

For a second, I just watched her—the way she always stood with her weight centered, steady, unshakable. The way she adjusted her glasses with one hand while scrolling with the other. Somehow, even stillness radiated competence from her.

She saw me standing in the hallway like I was trying to memorize the place. Her eyes softened immediately. "Hey, Miles," she said, a small smile spreading. "Walk with me?"

I followed her into the manager's office—the door half-open, sunlight cutting across the desk in a warm stripe. She gestured for me to close it behind us.

"So." She folded her arms gently, not crossing them like a barrier, but more like she was tucking herself in. "Cody told me you finally accepted the Texas job."

I nodded. "Yeah. I start in a few months."

For a moment, she just looked at me—that long, assessing, quietly affectionate gaze she saved for moments that mattered. The kind of look that made you feel seen, not judged.

"I figured this day was coming," she said softly. "Still doesn't make it easier."

I swallowed. "You've been... you've been one of the best parts of this whole year, Marge. I don't think I'd have made it without you."

She smiled—a real one, slow and warm. "Oh, I don't know about all that. But I sure am proud of you."

Something in my chest tightened. "Really?"

"Miles," she said, stepping closer, "you walked into this unit carrying more weight than anyone knew, and you still showed up every day. You cared, you worked harder than most, and you lifted up the people around you. That's what makes a good nurse—not perfection, not memorizing every detail in the books."

Her voice dipped, quieter. "You deserved better than what happened to you at the other hospital, and I'm damn glad you didn't let it end you."

I looked down, blinking hard. "I'm going to miss this place. Miss all of you guys."

"We're going to miss you too." She rested a hand on my shoulder—steady, reassuring, exactly the way a leader should be. "Texas is lucky to have you. And I mean that."

I nodded slowly. "I just... I wish I could take this unit with me."

She laughed, that bright, throaty Marge laugh that managed to shake the dust off a room. "Oh, trust me—half of us considered hiding in your U-Haul."

I laughed too, because I needed to. Then the moment settled.

Marge reached out her hand to shake mine—professional, respectful. I hugged her without thinking. She hugged me back without hesitation.

When we stepped apart, she cleared her throat lightly. "Go do great things, Miles. And don't forget—you earned every inch of where you're heading."

"I won't forget."

"Good." She opened the office door and nodded toward the hallway. "Now get your ass out there. Your shift isn't over yet."

I stepped back onto Trauma Drama, feeling something I hadn't felt in months—the bittersweet ache of leaving something good.

***

I sat on the edge of the couch in our living room with my phone pressed to my ear, staring at the half-packed boxes scattered across the floor. Monica was still in the bedroom taping up another box while I took a break to answer the call. Earl's voice came through warm and steady as always.

"So, son, you accepted the offer from Big City, right?"

I nodded, even though he couldn't see it. "Yeah. It's official. They want me to start next month."

Earl let out a low chuckle. "Well, I'll be damned. See? Told you you'd land on your feet."

I exhaled slowly. "I don't know, Earl. It's just... hard to let go. Colorado was supposed to be home. What if it's just more of the same?"

His tone softened the way only his could. "Listen to me, Miles. You been through hell and came out the other side standin'. Big City ain't Mountainton, and you ain't the same man who walked into that mess. You're stronger now. And folks are rootin' for you—me included."

I swallowed. "Earl, I don't want to start over again and get burned."

"Son, sometimes you gotta close one door to open another. That's life. You take that job, and you go show 'em what you're made of. And if things ever get rough, you call me. I'll be here."

A small laugh slipped out of me. "You really think it's going to be all right?"

"I don't think, I know. You got grit, Miles. You got heart. Texas is damn lucky to have you. Now go pack those boxes, get yourself some barbecue, and start livin' again."

Something in my chest loosened—a knot I'd been carrying so long, I forgot what it felt like not to hold it. "Thank you, Earl. For everything."

He chuckled. "Don't thank me yet. Just promise me one thing."

"What's that?"

"Give it a real shot. Don't look back over your shoulder the whole time. You're headed somewhere new. Act like it."

A breath caught in my throat. "Yeah. I promise."

"Good. Now go on, son. Everything's gonna be all right."

For the first time in a long time, I believed him.

***

As Murphy's law would have it, things got weird as my time was wrapping up. I was in the grocery store with Monica on one chilly night. She had had a craving for the drumstick ice cream cones after we stocked up on kale and berries, so we found ourselves in the frozen section.

I saw a figure standing to the side of me about six feet away in familiar scrub colors only known to the nurses working in the Mountainton Medical Center. I had burned my own set of those scrubs after I'd been let go, so I knew that burgundy color and logo very well. I glanced over and staring at me was none other than Sassy from That Unit.

Her hair was now orange, and she had a strange sparkle in her eyes. Her face lit up like an excited kid who saw their favorite friend they hadn't seen in a while. She smiled with her entire face—not in the bizarre fake way that Dakota and Josey did. She was so genuinely happy to see me, and she didn't hesitate to stop and focus in on me when she realized who I was.

"Hey!" she spoke.

I didn't feel hatred or anger that I honestly thought I would if ever in a position like this. I didn't want to curse at her or spit at her. I remembered how nice she was at first, and in this moment, she looked like she wanted to drop her shopping basket and hug me. I think I would have hugged her back if she had; it's strange to realize that.

"Hey," I said back, and I felt a mix of emotions sprinkled with the pain of the feeling of betrayal and the consequences I had suffered for her words and her actions.

She didn't hesitate. "How you been?!"

I replied, "Good. You?" I only looked at her when speaking and kept my focused gaze on the drumsticks and every letter of every word on an ice cream snickers bars box that I wasn't even going to buy.

"Good," she went on, and at that moment, I had no other words I could conjure to say to her. It seemed like she really wanted to say more.

"Well," she continued, perhaps knowing it was time to cut this short, "it's good to see you."

"Thanks. You too," I told her.

She walked away, and I didn't look at her any longer. I never saw her again.

Monica and I grabbed the drumsticks and started to make our way to the self-checkout. "Hon, who was that?" she asked.

"Remember Sassy, who I told you about?" I asked.

"*That* was her?!" Monica exclaimed. I nodded my head. "Well, you really wanted to show her mercy," she told me.

"Why do you say that?" I asked.

Monica explained, "If you had told me, it was her, I would have given her hell." We both laughed.

***

For one night, I wasn't the nurse who almost broke. I was just one of them. My friends and co-workers threw me a party at an awesome bowling alley with plenty of food and alcohol to boot. We didn't want to say goodbye, though as we all knew, it was coming fast.

The smell of pizza, shoe polish, and that faint chemical tang from the lanes hit me as soon as I stepped inside the bowling alley. Before I could even take in the neon lights or the clatter of pins, Cody's voice erupted. "MILESY! GET OVER HERE, BRO!"

He came charging toward me like he'd been shot out of a confetti cannon. Behind him, my Trauma Drama crew—Shelley waving a beer in the air, Jess laughing so hard she nearly dropped her mozzarella sticks, and the three Megs clustered near lane thirteen like some kind of benevolent coven.

"You guys did all this?" I asked, stunned.

"Hell yeah, we did," Cody said, slinging his arm around me. "You're not escaping us without a proper send-off. Thought we were gonna let you slip off quietly? Hell no."

The First Meg raised her glass. "To Miles—the only new grad who survived all three of our orientations!"

"Barely," the Second Meg added, grinning.

The Third Meg elbowed her. "Don't listen to her, Miles. You did great. Honestly, we're still arguing over which one of us trained you better."

That made the whole group laugh.

Jess gestured toward the snack-covered table. "We got your favorite lane. And before you ask—yes, we ordered extra nachos because we know you're emotional."

"I'm not emotional," I protested.

Cody shoved a bright orange bowling ball into my hands. "You teared up when the bartender asked for your ID."

"That was allergies," I said.

"Sure, it was," Shelley chimed in.

I threw the ball, and it curved awkwardly before tipping over one pin.

"One!" Cody shouted like I'd just scored the winning touchdown in the Super Bowl. "He's already ON FIRE!"

I doubled over laughing.

As we started the next round, Marge walked in carrying a tray of nachos the size of a small canoe. She set it down and gave me a look that was equal parts fondness and mild warning. "You better eat. And don't think being sentimental gets you out of bowling. I've got shoes on."

I grinned. "Wouldn't dream of it."

She stepped closer, lowering her voice just a little. "You doing okay?"

"Yeah. I'm just going to miss this."

Her eyes softened. "We're going to miss you too. But you're ready for this next chapter. You really are."

Before I could respond, Cody yelled from across four lanes, "HEY! MARGE! Quit stealing our boy!"

"Let's get a group picture!" Jess added.

The Megs scrambled together, Shelley grabbed her phone, and Jess held out an arm to pull me in.

I stood in the center as everyone piled around me. Cody's arm was around my neck. The Megs squeezed in on the other side. Jess and Shelley were laughing. Marge was smiling behind us.

The camera flashed. For a moment, the noise of the bowling alley faded. All I could feel was warmth, belonging, and family.

I had walked into this unit broken. Somehow, with these people—these chaotic, loud, beautiful people—I had learned how to breathe again. The goodbye was coming fast but tonight wasn't about leaving; it was about friendship and familial love.

***

On the morning of my last night shift, I was waiting to hand off my patients to the dayshift when I noticed a sales representative for a medical device company showing up to demonstrate some new wound care dressings for us. My stomach was in knots as I saw him from afar. I had never met him in person, but I knew his face so well, because I had seen it every week, sometimes multiple times a week in a picture on a desk.

Chad was Josey's husband, and I had seen his picture every time I had to be in her office for the progress meetings. He seemed like the nicest guy in the world, and of course with my current luck, I was the first nurse he managed to be close enough to greet and give a demonstration of the new goodies for our unit to use. I tucked my ID badge into one of my scrub pockets on my chest. I didn't think he would know my name, but I couldn't be sure.

Chad chatted me up about the new equipment and how it was going to help us provide better care for our patients. It was indeed, and had it been any other person, I would have chatted him up quicker and for longer. Something about this guy's genuine kindness and manners disarmed me enough to let him know I was on my way out to move to Texas. He expressed jealousy, especially if I went to Hip City, which is where everyone wants to move to down there.

Despite my efforts to be of lesser words, Chad really seemed to enjoy talking to me. He put out his hand and shook mine strongly. "I'm Chad," he said.

"Hey, Chad, I'm pleased to meet you," I told him with a smile. He looked puzzled as to why I didn't give him my name, but he didn't say anything and just smiled.

Chad's attention was quickly turned to two of my colleagues who had just appeared, and I let out a sigh of relief after he left to approach them. I knew the fast-approaching exit was coming at just the right time. It was tough for me to keep having run-ins like these and Mountainton was just too small.

***

The U-Haul was packed, and the house keys were left in the lockbox on the front door for our realtor to collect later that day. The sky was still black. I stood by the truck with my hands in my pockets, staring at the home we'd made for ourselves together.

Monica kissed our dogs and closed the door of the rental van, wiping her eyes with her sleeve. She walked over, her voice soft but steady. "You ready, hon?"

I tried to smile, but it faltered. "I don't know. Feels like I'm leaving a piece of myself here."

She reached for my hand and squeezed it tight. "We're not leaving anything behind that matters. We're taking us. That's all we need."

I looked at her, eyes shining. "I'm scared, hon. What if it's just more of the same? What if I can't do this again?"

She stepped closer, wrapping her arms around me. "You can. You already did, and you're not alone this time. I'll be right behind you."

I hugged her back, holding on as if it could stop time. "Promise me you'll call if you need anything—if the van breaks down, if the dogs get sick, if you just... need to hear my voice."

She laughed. "I promise. You promise me you'll pull over if you get tired. No heroics, okay?"

I nodded, finally managing a real smile. "No heroics."

She kissed my cheek, then stepped back, wiping her eyes again. "Let's go find out what's waiting for us."

I watched her climb into the van, the dogs barking excitedly in the back. She rolled down the window. "See you on the other side, babe."

I climbed into the U-Haul, heart pounding, and called back, "See you on the other side, hon."

The engines started and we pulled away from the curb. We drove in darkness of the super early morning to Big City, Texas. I watched the mountains fade in the rearview mirror as the sunrose, lighting them like a blessing I didn't deserve but accepted anyway.

For the first time since this all began, I felt peace.

And with it came something I never thought I'd reach:

Forgiveness.

I forgave them—not because they deserved it, but because I did.

And I let them go.

# GLOSSARY

**Abdominal Dressing** - A sterile bandage placed over a wound or surgical site on the abdomen to keep it clean and protected while it heals.

**Abdominal Pain** - Pain or discomfort anywhere in the belly area. It can range from mild to severe and often points to digestive problems.

**Antiemetic** - A medication used to stop or reduce nausea and vomiting.

**Assessment** - A nurse's evaluation of a patient's condition. This includes checking vital signs, asking questions, and making clinical observations.

**Beta Blockers (e.g.,** Metoprolol, Carvedilol) - Heart medications that slow the heart rate and lower blood pressure. Often used for heart disease, arrhythmias, and hypertension.

**Blood Cultures** - A test that checks a blood sample for bacteria or infection. It helps identify serious infections in the bloodstream.

**Blood Glucose Check** - A quick finger-stick test to measure sugar levels in the blood. Common for diabetic or critically ill patients.

**Bolus / Bolusing** - Giving fluids or medication quickly through an IV line, often in emergencies or when rapid action is needed.

**BP – Blood Pressure,** a measure of how hard blood pushes against artery walls. Often monitored closely in hospitalized patients.

**BSN – Bachelor of Science in Nursing,** a four-year nursing degree required for professional nursing practice.

**Bowel Obstruction / Small Bowel Obstruction** - A blockage in the intestines that stops food, gas, or stool from moving normally. Can be dangerous if not treated.

**Charting** - *Recording patient information in the medical record—critical for safe communication and care.*

**CNA – Certified Nursing Assistant, a** *healthcare worker who helps nurses by assisting patients with basic needs like bathing, moving, or eating.*

**Code Blue**- *A hospital emergency involving a patient in cardiac or respiratory arrest. Triggers a rapid life-saving response.*

**Crohn's Disease** - *A long-term inflammatory disease of the digestive system that causes abdominal pain, diarrhea, and flares.*

**Diarrhea** - *Frequent, loose stools caused by illness, infection, or digestive upset.*

**Dilaudid (Hydromorphone)** - *A strong opioid pain medication often used for severe pain or postoperative recovery.*

**Emergency Department** - **T***he hospital area where urgent and life-threatening conditions are treated.*

**EEO – Equal Employment Opportunity** - *The federal office that handles workplace discrimination concerns.*

**EKG – Electrocardiogram, a** *test that captures electrical activity of the heart to detect rhythm abnormalities or heart strain.*

**Enema (Soap-suds Enema)** - *A fluid inserted into the rectum to stimulate bowel movement, often used for constipation.*

**Famotidine** - *A medication that reduces stomach acid and treats heartburn.*

**Fluids (IV) / Lactated Ringer's Solution** - *Hydrating fluids given through a vein to help with low blood pressure, dehydration, or blood loss.*

**GI – Gastrointestinal, r***efers to the digestive organs: stomach, intestines, and related structures.*

**Glucometer** - *A handheld device that measures blood sugar.*

**Gown (Isolation Gown)** - Protective clothing worn by staff to prevent spreading or catching infection.

**Heparin** - A blood thinner given under the skin to prevent blood clots, especially for hospitalized or surgical patients.

**Hematoma** - A collection of blood under the skin or within tissue—often looks like a large, swollen bruise.

**ICU – Intensive Care Unit, a** hospital unit for the sickest patients needing constant monitoring and life-supporting treatments.

**Ileostomy / Ostomy Bag** - A surgically created opening in the abdomen where waste exits into an external pouch.

**IV – Intravenous, d**elivering medication or fluid directly into the bloodstream through a vein.

**LSD – Lysergic Acid Diethylamide, a recreational** hallucinogenic drug.

**MAR – Medication Administration Record, a** digital list showing all medications ordered and given to a patient.

**Medication Reconciliation / Medication Sheets** - Tools nurses use to double-check each drug's name, dose, purpose, and timing to prevent medication errors.

**Metoprolol** - A beta blocker used to lower heart rate and blood pressure.

**MRSA – Methicillin-Resistant** Staphylococcus aureus. A difficult-to-treat bacterial infection requiring special precautions.

**Narcotics (Opioids)** - Powerful pain medications such as oxycodone, hydrocodone, Percocet, Norco, and Dilaudid.

**Nasogastric Tube (NGT)** - A tube inserted through the nose into the stomach for feeding or draining stomach contents.

**Neutropenic Precautions** - Strict protection for patients with weak immune systems to prevent infection.

*NGT Suction / Gastric Decompression* - *Using suction to remove stomach contents when a patient has a bowel obstruction or severe nausea.*

**Opioids** - *Another term for narcotics—strong pain medications.*

**Ostomy Appliance** - *The equipment used to collect waste from a surgically created abdominal opening.*

**PCA – Patient-Controlled Analgesia,** *a pump that lets patients press a button to self-dose pain medication safely.*

**Percocet** - *A combination pain medication (oxycodone + acetaminophen).*

**Percutaneous Line / IV Access** - *A tube inserted through the skin into a vein for medications or fluids.*

**PTSD – Post-traumatic stress disorder, a** *trauma-related condition triggered by past events.*

**QT Interval** - *A measure of the heart's electrical rhythm on an EKG. If prolonged, it increases risk of dangerous arrhythmias.*

**RT – Respiratory Therapist,** *healthcare professionals who manage breathing treatments, ventilators, and airway emergencies.*

**SCI – Spinal Cord Injury**. A serious condition that results from damage to the spinal cord, leading to partial or complete loss of movement, sensation, or other bodily functions below the level of injury. These patients often require specialized nursing care, rehabilitation, and long-term support.

*__Step-Down__* - *__A__ level of care between an ICU and a regular hospital floor.*

*__Simethicone__* - *Medication that relieves gas and bloating.*

*__Suction Canister__* - *A container that collects drainage or stomach contents when suction is used.*

*__Subcutaneous Injection__* - *A shot given into the fatty tissue under the skin.*

*__Telemetry (Tele)__* - *A monitoring system that tracks a patient's heart rhythm continuously.*

*__Tele-sitter__* - *A remote camera-based monitoring system used for patient safety.*

*__Urinary Catheter__*- *A tube placed into the bladder to drain urine.*

**Ventilation / Respiratory Support** - Any treatment that helps a patient breathe, such as oxygen therapy or mechanical ventilation.

*__Voltaren (Diclofenac Gel)__* - *A topical anti-inflammatory medication used to treat muscle or joint pain.*

*__Zofran (Ondansetron)__* - *A powerful anti-nausea medication that can affect heart rhythm in some patients.*

# AUTHOR'S NOTE

This book is, at its core, a piece of my heart. Writing it meant reopening wounds I thought had long since scarred over. It was born during a time when I was trying to make sense of what had happened to me—when I was learning, sometimes painfully, how to heal.

My first year in nursing nearly broke me. I wrote these pages while working through trauma exposure therapy, trying to find meaning in the chaos and hurt. If you've ever felt alone, doubted, or pushed aside—especially in a place where you were supposed to belong—I want you to know I see you. You're not alone.

The story you've just read is fiction, but it's stitched together from real memories, emotions, and moments that left their mark. I didn't set out to write a perfect record of events. Instead, I wanted to capture the emotional truth of what it feels like to be silenced, to be doubted, and to fight for your place in a world that sometimes seems determined to push you out.

What got me through were the small kindnesses—the people who chose empathy when it would have been easier to look away. For every person who caused harm, there were others who quietly tried to do the right thing. This book is for them, too.

If you're a nurse, a healthcare worker, a veteran, or anyone who's been bullied, harassed, or hurt in the workplace: what happened to you matters. It doesn't define your worth, and it doesn't get to decide your future. I hope my story helps you feel seen, and maybe a little less alone.

Thank you for reading. Please, take care of yourself. You deserve it.

— T.A. Benson

# ABOUT THE AUTHOR

T. A. Benson was born in Mississippi and grew up in a small town reminiscent of the one in *Footloose*. In his youth, he found solace in art, guitar, and film, dreaming of a future in Hollywood. However, economic challenges and the events of September 11, 2001, led him to join the U.S. Army, where he served as an infantryman during the Iraq War. After sustaining a traumatic brain injury, he transitioned to a career in healthcare, becoming a respiratory therapist and later a nurse. His journey through adversity, including battling PTSD and overcoming professional challenges, has shaped his resilient and compassionate approach to life. He now channels his experiences into his writing, offering readers a unique blend of authenticity and inspiration.

# THROUGH THE FIRE

9 798330 449071